D1433743

22369

QUEEN MARGARET COLLEGE LIBRARY

Please return book by date stamped below

2 5 NOV 1982
1 8 FEB 1983
2 0 APR 1983
1 2 NOV 1984
CANCELLED
CANCELLED 1986
CANCELLED
CANCELLED
CANCELLED
5 MAY 1998
CANCELLED

27 JUN
4 DEC 1978

1979
1979

AR 1980
AY 1980

6 MAY 1980
AY 1980

JUL

OCT

19 DE

10 MA 1982
4 OC 1982

GOOD HOUSEKEEPING
Complete Book of
DECORATING

Withdrawn from
Queen Margaret University Library

QUEEN MARGARET COLLEGE LIBRARY

GOOD HOUSEKEEPING

Complete Book of

DECORATING

By Mary Kraft

Good Housekeeping Books   New York

GOOD HOUSEKEEPING BOOKS

Editor MINA WHITE MULVEY
Art Director WILLIAM LEFT
Art Consultant JOHN ENGLISH
Senior Editor JOHN WALSH
Copy Editor JUANITA G. CHAUDHRY
Assistant to Art Director LYNN THOMPSON

FOR GOOD HOUSEKEEPING MAGAZINE

Editor WADE H. NICHOLS
Executive Editor JOHN B. DANBY
Managing Editor BENSON SRERE
Art Director BERNARD SPRINGSTEEL
Director, The Institute WILLIE MAE ROGERS

Copyright © MCMLXXI by the Hearst
Corporation. Manufactured in the United
States of America. All rights reserved.
No part of this book may be reproduced in
any manner whatsoever without the
written permission of the publisher.
ISBN 0-87851-005-2. Library of Congress
Catalog Number 71-137515.

contents

the first step
IS TO THINK ABOUT THE WAY YOU LIVE   9

color
IS THE KEYNOTE OF ANY DECORATING PLAN   34

pattern and texture
GIVE WALLS AND WALL COVERINGS, FLOORS, FURNITURE,
AND FABRIC NEW DIMENSIONS   62

floors
LAY THE GROUNDWORK FOR GOOD DECORATING   78

furniture
IS FOR COMFORT AND FOR STYLE   96

planning
CAN SAVE YOU TIME, MONEY, AND MISTAKES   112

lighting
MAKES YOUR DECORATING SCHEME COME ALIVE   128

window treatments—
MAKE THEM FOCAL POINTS OF THE ROOM'S DECOR   142

accessories
GIVE A ROOM CHARM AND INDIVIDUALITY   166

table settings
PROVIDE A DAILY CHANCE TO BE CREATIVE   186

storage
LETS YOU KEEP THINGS UNDER CONTROL   200

tricks
PROFESSIONAL DECORATORS USE AND YOU CAN COPY   212

do-it-yourself
IDEAS FOR EVERY ROOM IN THE HOUSE   224

appendix
PLACES TO VISIT • BOOKS FOR FURTHER READING
PHOTOGRAPHERS' CREDITS • INTERIOR DESIGNERS' CREDITS •
OTHER CREDITS • FURNITURE CUTOUTS • PLANNING GRID   242

index
251

GOOD HOUSEKEEPING

Complete Book of

DECORATING

the first step

IS TO THINK ABOUT
THE WAY YOU LIVE

Decorating your home is a little like falling in love: It's full of excitement and anticipation and delight. And while, on the one hand, it sets you to daydreaming, on the other it makes you more aware of everything around you—of colors and textures and shapes, and of how these can be combined to produce exactly the effect you want, whether you're slipcovering a chair or decorating a whole house.

Still, these pleasurable feelings are sometimes tinged with doubt. How do you make a choice among the many possibilities that are open to you? How do you even know what all the possibilities are? It's true that a wrong choice here is one of life's lesser disasters. But it is a disaster nonetheless, the more deplorable because it is so easily prevented.

For decorating is not the mystery it is sometimes made out to be. If you can put together an attractive costume—a dress, a scarf, a pair of shoes—you'll have no trouble making your home a pleasant and comfortable place to live in, one that will please your family and impress your friends. The tools you need are simply a few general principles and a lot of specific facts. This book is designed to give you both, plus a look at the many resources available to you whatever project you decide to undertake. But that's not all.

The best of all possible ways of decorating, for you and your family, is a way that is entirely and individually yours. Consequently, the book's main purpose is to help you develop confidence in your own taste and judgment. It is here that the illustrations can be especially helpful. First of all, they cover a great variety of life styles, from that of the young (and not-so-young) marrieds with great ideas but no money, to those of couples with a taste, and pocketbook, for fine antiques. Among them you are sure to find several that more or less reflect the way you like to live.

But more than that, these pictures are planned to teach you a new way of looking, to train your eye to see the rules behind all good decorating. *Those* rules are not cut-and-dried dos and don'ts that may or may not apply to your particular situation. They result from a natural feeling for the relationships among the many elements—color, pattern, texture, and so forth—that combine to produce a handsome room, apartment, or house. Once you learn to spot these relationships and apply them to your own problems, decorating your home will become the exhilarating and successful experience it's supposed to be.

Begin at the beginning

You start where every good professional decorator does—by finding out the needs of the client. *You* are your own client, but that doesn't mean you can scant the hard work of analyzing how you and your family go about your lives. The most stunning decorating scheme in the world is no good if it won't stand up to the onslaughts of daily living, or if it requires more maintenance than you can give it.

A fundamental need is for each member of the family to have some degree of privacy to pursue a hobby or special interest. A second essential is that the rooms the family shares—living room, dining room, family room, kitchen—be planned first for day-to-day living, *then* for entertaining. But after these basics are established, the questions come thick and fast.

Think about the way you live

Is your home one where there is a place for everything and everything is (or should be) in its place? Or does your family live all over the house, with toys, books, and magazines everywhere contributing to a look of cheerful clutter? When the weather permits, do you do a good deal of living outdoors? Is your way of life child-oriented or directed

If you're in love with the formal look
that implies gracious living,
this room may appeal to you. Antique furnishings
include a tilt-top table, banister-back armchair,
and a Sheraton sofa; still more antiques
dress the mantel in an asymmetrical arrangement
of a pillar-and-scroll clock flanked by a tole tray,
brass candlesticks, and a box once used as a tea caddy.
A similar effect could be achieved with reproductions.

*Contemporary
is a way of living . . .*

clutter-free and easy to maintain,
with form following function
and every material chosen
for its basic beauty.
On these pages, an apartment living room
with a versatile arrangement
of simple furniture designed
for conversation, for lounging,
or for easy and casual service of meals.
Two versions of a boldly colored plaid,
larger for the area rug, smaller
for the divan and oversized ottomans,
unite the grouping of furniture.
Floor-to-ceiling curtains
of sheer yellow suggest sunlight
on the dimmest day,
provide sufficient privacy at night.
A simple arrangement of Fuji mums
and ivy repeats the color scheme
of the room. The contemporary painting
and Mexican terra-cotta figure
add individual touches.

toward adult interests? Or is it a happy combination of both? How much entertaining do you do, and what kind? Does your family do things together, or is each one of you a rugged individualist? What are the main traffic patterns in your home? Is it a reasonably permanent abode, or do you expect to move on in a few years?

This is just a sampling of the kinds of questions you should know the answers to before you even begin collecting swatches. A decorating scheme is a good one only if it works. And to work it must add to the pleasure and comfort of every member of the household. Discuss your plans with your husband and children. You may find that they can contribute ideas and insights you have overlooked.

A major factor in your plans, of course, will be how much money you have to spend. There never seems to be enough. But remember that money is a function of time: the longer the period you stretch your efforts over, the more funds you'll have to work with. That's why it's important to have a master plan before you buy so much as an end table. Its style and scale should be right for the room that at present exists only in your mind but eventually will be a reality.

Sometimes necessity proves to be a virtue and saves you from making costly mistakes you'll have to live with for years. Go slow while you explore your tastes in furnishings. You don't, in the meantime, have to live out of orange crates. You can experiment with inexpensive used pieces, painted in gay colors; director's chairs; daybeds heaped with bright pillows, and other low-cost stand-ins. You'll find many attractive examples in this book.

Once you know exactly what you want, buy furnishings of enduring quality and style, even if you can manage only one piece at a time.

Your home is your setting

No woman ever thinks of her home as a stage set. And yet it's true that you are complemented by your surroundings, just as actresses are. It is worthwhile, therefore, particularly where color is concerned, to give a thought to what kind of decorating scheme is becoming to you personally. That is not as vain as it sounds. To your guests, and even to your own family, the mistress of the house is an element in its decorative effect. Your own living room should not upstage you, clash

Appealingly traditional but comfortable,
and with formal overtones, French provincial
is another favorite life style. Fabric
is the decorative starting point in this room,
covering walls and draping windows
with the same authentic pattern.
Strips of molding added to longer walls
create a paneled effect. Secondary colors
in the fabric are used for sofa and chairs.

If you love to cook,
let your kitchen be a showcase
for your most treasured
cooking aids. On these pages
are different approaches
to kitchen decoration,
each reflecting the personality
of the owner. At right,
the mood is nostalgic,
everything is within easy reach—
copper and iron cooking
and baking utensils, even
a row of spices in ordinary
glass jars—all enhancing
the natural brick walls
and wooden counters
of this early American kitchen.
On the opposite page,
a contemporary-minded cook
displays only a few objects,
both useful and decorative,
against sleek surfaces.
On a background
of washable vinyl wall covering,
from left to right: a copper mold
above a framed painting, a clock,
bright red cooking pots,
and antique utensils
mounted on a wooden panel.
All else is tidily stored
in cupboards.

with you, or put you—literally—in an unfavorable light. You and your home should show each other off.

Keep that thought in the back of your mind while you're decorating, but don't let it run away with you. Comfort should never be sacrificed to appearance, and fortunately today it doesn't have to be. Furniture, even that which reproduces older styles, is scaled to the proportions of modern rooms—and modern anatomy. New fibers and finishes make once-too-vulnerable colors and textures usable in almost any situation. For a minimum of maintenance, investigate drip-dry curtains, wipe-clean vinyl upholstery, easily maintained flooring, and other time and work savers.

Style is a way of life

When you look closely at your and your family's needs, likes and dislikes, activities, entertainment patterns, and so forth, you'll find that they already suggest the general outlines of a decorating plan. That is to be expected. All the various ways of decorating grew up in response to the demands of particular life styles.

If you like comfort, informality, a feeling of warmth and unpretentiousness, you'll find yourself naturally turning to decorating schemes that express those qualities. In furniture, you may be drawn to early American, modern, Mediterranean, or any of a dozen other designs that grew up at different times and in different places but have essentially the same appreciation for the fundamental good things of life. As you study various possibilities and the fabrics, colors, accessories that go with them, the deciding factor in your choice may be the emotional appeal of a particular style.

Clean-limbed modern, for example, has a sparseness that repels some

If your way of life is casual . . .

and you delight
in putting old things
to new uses, here's
a way of adding warmth
to today's furniture.
In this suburban
family room,
a collection
of old ironware
decorates the brick
fireplace wall;
an old school desk,
now painted bright red,
enchants the children;
the old parlor stove,
at lower right, serves
as a lamp table.
But practicality
is not sacrificed
to nostalgia;
the raised hearth,
with its hand-hewn
overbeam, is handy
for informal cooking;
the sectioned top
of the butler's tray
coffee table lifts off,
to be loaded
with drinks and snacks
from the nearby kitchen;
the sofa converts
to a bed, making room
for a guest.

people. To others it has the beauty and authority of a moon rocket and is just right for the age in which we live. The spirit of early American, on the other hand, is one of a distinctive coziness, plus a nostalgic harking back to earlier values.

It's interesting to recall that this mood was there from the beginning. The early settlers in this country made their houses and furniture conform, so far as they were able, to models they remembered from home. In the Deerfield Museum, in western Massachusetts, there are cases filled with seventeenth-century English china. It is there because the first pioneer women, setting out for the wilderness from the relative safety of the coastal settlements, insisted on carrying these reminders of a gentler way of life in the saddlebags of the horses.

Temperament makes the difference

At the opposite extreme from the homey feeling of a New England kitchen or a New Mexican adobe house are styles modeled after those favored by the aristocracy in periods when life was more leisurely and more ordered, at least for the upper classes. These too vary widely in origin and flavor, from the rococo exuberance of the Louis XV period to the simple, classic lines of Biedermeier (opposite). Good modern furnishings, because of the purity of their design, can also be used in a formal setting, where they take their cue from their surroundings.

What all these styles have in common is an ordered elegance that calls for a corresponding way of life, dignified, gracious, and unhurried. The family that likes to entertain formally, that makes a habit of traditions like afternoon tea, that enjoys the pleasures of conversation and other quiet pursuits often finds itself happiest in this kind of setting. It can be re-created authentically with fine antiques or, at more moderate cost, by using the excellent reproductions of earlier styles that are now available.

Between the most formal and the most informal ways of decorating

Living with elegance can be achieved
in the smallest room, as in the 11′ x 15′6″ apartment
living room at left. The trick is to use
small furniture, a mirror or two,
see-through glass lamps, and a minimum of pattern.
Other points worth noticing: broad bands
of blue ribbon trim readymade window shades,
sofa pillows, and the felt-covered table
in the foreground; the antique Biedermeier table,
mirror and chair create a focal point in a room
without architectural interest. Another plus:
Everything here can be adapted to other rooms
when the family moves on to larger quarters.

The kind of family
that finds much of its fun
at home might want to consider
converting unused space
in attic or basement
into a playroom for all ages.
Above, chairs are from junk shops,
banquettes are homemade. Pillows,
cushions, are of easy-care vinyl,
serving double duty
as extra seating on the floor.

there is an almost infinite series of gradations and variations. Just as modern styling isn't confined to casual settings, so a fondness for the traditional look doesn't mean you must force your family's behavior into an unnaturally rigid mold.

Some period styles vary in degree of formality according to the patterns and textures used with them. Brocades, velvets, silks and satins, in classic patterns and traditional motifs, give a room a grander air than one in which fabrics equally appropriate but sturdier— printed cottons and linens or wools, perhaps—are used.

Nor is there any law of decorating that says you must furnish a traditional room in a completely traditional way. Some of the most interesting decorating schemes, as well as the most comfortable, are achieved by mixing periods or combining the old and the new.

In the room on the opposite page, for example, the classic lines of the table and chairs, French Empire in inspiration, complement the

simple raised hearth, contrast with the delicate curves of the rococo china cabinet. On page 35, a bright nontraditional color on a traditional French provincial chair provides a welcome element of surprise. Taking the opposite tack, houses that are entirely contemporary, from architecture to furnishings, may be mellowed by the addition of a few antiques. An old sleigh bed, a primitive painting, or an elaborately carved chest may add just the touch of piquancy a modern room needs.

Technically, an item must be at least 100 years old to be called an "antique." As generally used, however, the word means anything old and interesting, particularly items made before mass-production methods became widespread. Very old and/or very fine pieces are fabulously expensive. But there is also a vast quantity of old things, some of them badly in need of loving care, accessible to collectors with limited funds.

If you have a fondness for leisurely dining, you'll want a room for it that promotes conversation and serenity. Soothing green predominates in the room above. A handsome collection of unmatched pieces of furniture adds interest. The same room also serves for bridge, other games, all cheered by the glowing fire.

*If you
delight
in the heritage*

of stately living that dates
back to the early colonists,
this room is worthy
of careful study.
On these pages,
faithful adaptations
of the still popular
Queen Anne style,
now slightly smaller in size
for use in modern homes.
Pull-out shelves
on the tea table are serving
their original purpose
of holding candles.
The chandelier is typical
of the period, as is
the balanced arrangement
on the mantel. Table lamps
at either side of the fireplace
have been converted
from antique candelabra.
Built-in bookshelves
in the mellowed paneled walls
hold a collection of old volumes;
patterned rug repeats
the room's subtle color scheme.

If you like the look antiques can give, don't confine your search to dealers' offerings. Seek out secondhand boutiques and junk, thrift, and antique shops; haunt Salvation Army stores, white elephant sales, and charity bazaars; watch for auction and estate sales. Learn how to care for old furniture, and how to refinish it if necessary (see page 243 for books that tell you how).

Good taste is made, not born

Faced with the necessity of choosing among so many possibilities in decorating your home, it's comforting to remember that nobody is *born* with the instinctive ability to make all the right decisions. Taste is the product of knowledge, and in this field that mostly comes from keeping your eyes open. Nature, for one, can be a great teacher. Is there any more exquisite design than that of a shell or a leaf, any color combination more subtle than a fading sunset's hues? Learning to notice and appreciate the line, proportion, and harmony in the natural world around you will teach you to reject the second-rate in manmade things.

An aptitude for tasteful decorating can also be cultivated in other ways:

• Study period rooms in museums and historical societies, not with the idea of slavishly reproducing them, but to experience the authentic flavor of past decorating styles.

• Visit, when you can, the great historic houses that have been restored to their original beauty. A list of these is given on page 242.

• Watch for house tours in your area. More and more frequently, for the benefit of charity, private homes and apartments of distinction are being opened to the public.

• Check the programs of local colleges, women's clubs, and other groups for special events featuring speakers on home furnishings and related subjects. If you yourself belong to a club, ask your program chairman to investigate the many films on decorating available from film libraries or from firms in the home furnishings field.

• Look at model rooms in furniture and department stores. Although some of these are simply merchandise displays, others have been planned by skillful decorators and are well worth careful study.

• Start your own file of ideas. Many manufacturers of paint, wallpaper, furniture, rugs, and other products offer informative booklets and kits. Collect these, together with pictures, color chips, and fabric swatches that appeal to you. Play with them a little, trying out various combinations just to see how they look.

• If you have the opportunity, go on the plant tours offered by many firms in the home furnishings field (write to the Department of

TEXT CONTINUED ON PAGE 32

A young outlook and a modest budget demand crisp
and lively decoration. Here, one strong color
covers sofa bed and floor; other colors are neutral.
Pillows repeat colors in the vibrant wall hanging.
The table in foreground also serves for dining.

Remodeling an attic is a familiar way to add
space in an old house. Here, different ways of doing it:
Opposite: In a newly created bedroom, family relics
and handed-down furniture, united by a documentary
wall covering, produce a peaceful retreat.
Matching fabric, trimmed with fringe, is used for shades.

Above: In this very active family room, one wall
has been replaced by windows. Contemporary furniture,
vinyl surfaces and fabrics, factory-finished paneling,
all assure easy maintenance and resistance
to hard use. Snack-bar stools are movable, for use
as extra seating anywhere. A shaggy rug
provides color inspiration for pillows and upholstery.

Below: If you welcome neighbors who drop in for a chat
at any hour, create a cozy corner for happy breaks
in your daily routine. Here, a sunny bow window,
left uncurtained for maximum sunlight and view,
acts as a greenhouse. The arms of the chairs hold snacks.

Right: If you live an active life in the city, on the go
from early morning until late at night, you may desire
serene formality in your living room. In this town house,
accessories gathered from all over the world
soften the room's formal effect, have their own interest.
Modern rug fits perfectly into the period mood.

Economic Development in your state capital for a list of industrial tours in your state). Actually seeing how glass, china, silver, furniture, floor coverings, and so forth are made can help you distinguish the good from the bad or the simply mediocre.

• Read other books on decorating. For suggestions, see page 243.

Take it step by step

Now that you have an overall view of the things to think about before you begin your decorating project, you're ready to plunge into the details. Because color is the single strongest component of any room, the following chapter explains its basic rules and how to use them to create exciting color schemes. Next comes a consideration of pattern and texture, the two other general aspects of furnishings and the backgrounds that set them off. Only then does it make sense to explore the many possibilities in floor coverings, furniture, lighting, window treatments, accessories, and all the other specific elements that go into a complete decorating scheme. One tip: Refer frequently to the unique pictorial Index (pages 251 to 256). It will lead you to further references, scattered throughout the book, to topics that arouse your special interest.

Right: Comfort and handsome contemporary style are both available to the woman who wants to cut housework to a minimum. Flooring is of stone-patterned, embossed linoleum; oak paneling adds character without care; a wide band of molding hides lighting fixtures, and a traverse rod for drip-dry curtains spans the window wall beneath the clerestory window.

Left: In a crisp, colorful breakfast area facing the street, the privacy problem is solved by an unusual window treatment: cafe curtains on a brass rod shield the table; sheer draperies add a softening effect; a window shade provides control of daylight, night privacy. An antique wall clock and a reproduction of an old lighting fixture add charm.

color

IS THE KEYNOTE
OF ANY DECORATING PLAN

Used with imagination, color can make a good decorating scheme a triumph. Used badly, it can turn the same combination of ingredients into a disaster. The difference between the two is a matter of knowing the rules of color well enough to produce harmonious relationships at whatever level of intensity you choose. Delicate or vivid, clear or shadowy, restrained to one key or modulating into several, an effective color scheme is guided by the same basic considerations. Some of these have to do with the physical aspects of color, others with its psychological effects.

Color is dependent upon light

Without light there can *be* no color; what we see as color is simply light of a certain wave length arriving at the eye. White light contains all wave lengths, but most objects absorb many of these. Depending upon which ones they reflect, we see them as blue, green, violet, or any of a myriad other hues.

Varying qualities and intensities of light can make the same color look different. That's why, in planning any decorating scheme, it's vital to view the colors selected—in paint chips, rug samples, fabric swatches—in the room in which they are to be used, under both day and night lighting. ·

This is particularly important for large areas, such as floors and walls, where color reflects upon color. Remember that in the finished room, this reflecting quality will make whatever hue you choose for

TEXT CONTINUED ON PAGE 40

Blue and white, sparked by citrus yellow, makes a brilliant color scheme. Floral-patterned draperies and upholstery (all fabrics are linen) underline traditional character of the furnishings. Flowers, ash trays, gold-framed mirror, echo hue of the twin Louis XV open-arm chairs.

34

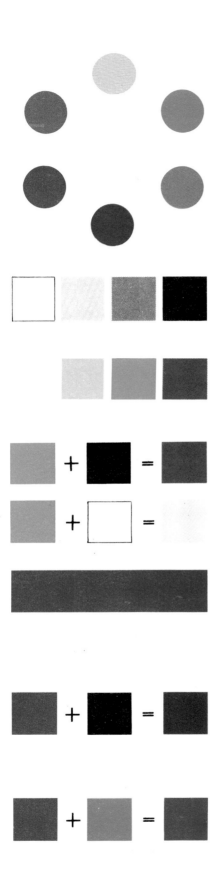

COLOR HAS A VOCABULARY

This is what is commonly called a color wheel or color circle. Some wheels contain many more colors than are shown here, but this one gives the basic six: yellow, green, blue, violet, red, and orange.

HUES are simply colors: yellow, red, blue, and so on—everything except black, white, grey, and their mixtures.

NEUTRALS are black, white, grey, and greyed tones such as beige or cream.

VALUE refers to the lightness or darkness of a color—to light blue, dark blue, and the many gradations between.

SHADES are hues with black added, making them darker in value.

TINTS are hues with white added, making them lighter in value.

INTENSITY refers to the brightness or dullness of a color. Pure hues are brightest, most intense.

You can lower the intensity of a hue by adding white or black, or by adding some of the hue's complement. Look at the color wheel above: colors directly opposite each other on the wheel are complementary.

To grey a color, add a bit of its complement—a small amount can make the color softer, subtler. Too much can make the color very dull or cause it to lose most of its original hue.

Hundreds of colors can be made by mixing pure hues and tints and shades of hues.

WARM OR COOL COLORS

Some colors appear warm—the reds, yellow, and red-violets. Others appear cool—the blues, many greens, and blue-violets. Some colors, like green, can seem either warm or cool: yellow-greens seem warm, blue-greens seem cool. A touch of blue added to white will make it seem even icier; a touch of yellow will mellow white.

The intensity and value of a color also affect its apparent "temperature." Intense colors appear warmer than dull ones.

LIGHT MAKES A DIFFERENCE

Intense colors appear brighter in strong light or sunshine. One by one the colors seem to disappear as the light fades, until finally you see only the light colors or white.

Experiment with a paint sample of a color you like:

• Look at it in a room where you might use the color; note the effect on it of surrounding colors.

• Look at it on a dull day—and again when the sun is shining.

• Shut out the sunlight and turn on a lamp to see what happens to the color.

• Look at it at several locations in the room, with the light striking it from different angles.

Artificial light often tends to change the hue as you see it. It can make a pink tablecloth appear violet, or give a blue bedspread a greenish color. This is important to remember when shopping. Store lighting is different from home lighting, and home lighting varies greatly. Both are different from natural light. It's best to collect swatches that you can examine under various lighting conditions.

PLAN FOR COLOR HARMONY

There are three main plans for using color, and they apply whether you are working with a table setting, an accessory grouping, or a room. Each plan can be equally good if the color values, intensities, and amounts are chosen with care. If they are not, the plan could be so intense that you could not live with it, so intense that the colors would vibrate. Or it could be so bland that it totally lacked impact.

A one-color plan (monochromatic) uses several values (tints and shades) of one color, some bright, some dull.

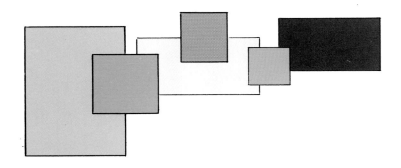

A related color plan (analogous) uses colors that lie next to each other on the color wheel, including their tints, shades, and intermediate hues.

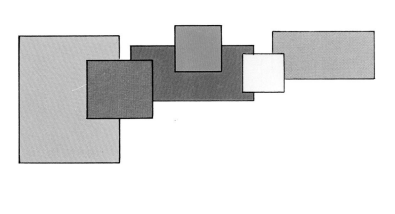

A complementary color plan uses colors opposite each other on the color wheel. Red and green are one example, a scheme that is used by nature in roses, tulips, carnations, and many other red flowers. Because cool colors are less active than warm ones, you might prefer a complementary scheme that uses smaller amounts of the bright, warm colors, larger amounts of the cool.

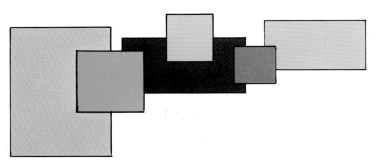

COLORS AFFECT ONE ANOTHER

The same color can appear quite different in different surroundings, a fact to keep in mind when you are shopping. The sketches at the right show what happens when orange is placed first against a yellow-green background, then against blue, and finally against lavender. Against the yellow-green, it looks darker, against the blue, more intense, while the lavender background makes it appear less intense.

Colors affect one another in other ways too. Some combinations sharpen the impact of each color contained in them; others make the component colors look drab, faded, or gaudy. Whenever two or more colors are to be used in a room, study them carefully together to see whether they will bring out the best in each other. Just as a brown dish for scrambled eggs or a dull green one for sliced tomatoes can make these foods seem special ones, so the right color backgrounds can enhance your furnishings and accessories.

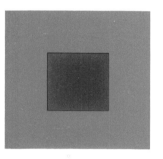

EXPERIMENT WITH COLOR

Learn to use the vocabulary of color; it will help you in everything from mixing paints to analyzing color schemes you would like to copy. Experiment with the various color plans to gain confidence in selecting colors for many purposes—clothes and appetizing-looking meals as well as decorating schemes. Recognize that color changes in different kinds of light, that each color is affected by surrounding ones, and that you must experiment in order to find satisfying combinations. Above all, realize the importance of total planning—that a beautiful table setting, a flattering costume, or an attractive room is a harmonious whole and not just an unrelated assembly of parts.

Exploring color is an exciting experience. Learning to see it in everyday things is rewarding; learning how to use it is a challenge.

large areas seem much deeper in value than the small sample you hold in your hand. Walls, especially, bounce color back and forth like Ping Pong balls.

Color has temperature

Psychologically speaking, color can be either warm or cool. The effect, of course, is purely emotional; oranges and reds and yellows don't really raise the temperature of a room. What they do do is make it *look* warmer. Blues, blue-greens, and blue-violets have the opposite effect, creating a cool and tranquil mood.

This kind of color association seems to be a heritage from man's kinship with nature. White seems cool because it is the color of newly fallen snow, blue recalls the icy depths of mountain lakes, green signals a leafy haven from the burning sun. Just as logically, the colors of fire and of the sun-warmed earth, from yellow to brown and deepest red, seem warm or hot.

This quality of color can be used to counter the effect of a room's exposure. A room facing north or northeast gets little or no direct sunlight, and the light it does receive is blue in tone. Such a room may look chilly and forbidding unless it is splashed with warm color. Pale yellow walls, for example, will have an immediate cheering effect, with the additional benefit of suggesting the missing sunlight. In contrast, rooms with a southern or southwestern exposure are flooded with hot yellow light for most of the day. They may need the cooling effect of blues or greens, in shades dark enough to absorb some of the excess brilliance.

Climate is another consideration in choosing a color scheme. Warm colors can ease the chilling psychological effect of long and dreary winters, cool ones the oppressive feeling of endless heat. Significantly, white walls are great favorites in tropical climates, while in cooler northern countries the warm tones of wood paneling are popular.

Color can affect size

Perhaps as an extension of their emotional temperature, colors also have a temperamental effect. The warm ones tend to seem exciting and active, the cool ones restful and restrained. This quality of color also affects our perception of size: tranquil colors can make a room look larger, while vibrant ones may seemingly shrink its dimensions

Chinese red, so named for a characteristically Oriental lacquer, and mandarin gold predominate in this rich color scheme. Ever since the fourteenth century, when the first European travelers returned from the East bringing treasures of porcelain and silk, Chinese design has had a strong impact on Western furnishings. Here, chairs, coffee table, and red chest all trace their ancestry to China.

because more seems to be going on.

The intensity and value of the colors used have an even greater effect on the apparent size of a room. Pale colors retreat, leading the eye into the distance. Strong, vivid colors jump out toward you. That is why a room whose walls are white or pastel seems much larger than the same-size room painted a deep or a bold color. (Still, if you prefer intense colors to pale ones, use them. Better a small room with character than a larger-looking one that seems insipid.)

You can use the eye-fooling effect of color to change the proportions of a room as well as its size. A long narrow room will look less like a hallway if you paint the short walls in a bold, advancing color. To tame an awkwardly high ceiling, paint it several shades darker than the walls; it will immediately seem to descend. White or a pale tint of the wall color will make a low ceiling look higher. An effective trick is to paint the ceiling of an entryway a very dark color, that of the adjoining living room a very light one. The contrast will make the living room seem especially large and airy.

Use a color contrasting with that of the main expanse of wall if you want to draw attention to architectural features, such as moldings, dadoes, or fireplace mantels. But if the room is too broken up by these, or if they are ugly or undistinguished, paint them the same color as the walls and they will tend to disappear.

Three ways of using color

These color rules can be applied to whatever color scheme you choose. As explained on page 38, there are three basic types: one-color, related, and complementary. If you have a strong preference for a particular color, in many varying shades and tints, the one-color plan might be a good one for you. A neutral one-color scheme is a safe choice for those who are uncertain about their color preferences: it permits unlimited experimentation with various colors as accents. The room on the opposite page is a handsome example of what can be done with such a scheme. A different choice of flowers and of other small accessories can alter the whole mood. Instead of the tulip-red, imagine the yellow of springtime daffodils and mimosa, or the bright zinnia colors of summer, and you will get the idea.

Using a related color plan, you might combine yellow, orange, and red, as in the room on the previous page, or, going the other way around the color wheel, yellow, green, and blue, as on pages 50 and 51. A good example of a complementary plan is the red-green room, page 55.

Whichever plan you elect, the first step is to choose your major color, the one to be used on the largest expanses, such as the floor or walls. Next select a secondary color (or shade) for the second largest areas, perhaps the upholstery or drapery fabrics. Then add a few other colors, in small amounts, for accent in accessories.

There are so many possibilities in working out a color plan that it is sometimes difficult to choose among them. One way to start is to

Black and white, stark opposites, are used with style in a dining room furnished with chrome-and-glass table and chairs. Drawings above the white-painted buffet continue the color scheme.

visualize your major color as a shell, or setting, for family activities. Is it becoming to you personally, or to whoever will be the room's main occupant? Does it suit the room's function? Is it compatible with the mood you want the room to have—formal or informal, warm or cool, intense or tranquil?

If the color you have chosen satisfies you on all these points, you might consider using it, in closely adjacent values of light or dark, for ceiling, walls, floor, *and* window draperies. Furniture and accessories can be in related or contrasting colors, or, if you prefer the one-color

Here, an expanse of white makes a perfect background for the use of brilliant color in accessories, such as pillows that can be changed when your color mood varies.

look, in more widely differentiated values of the same color.

To avoid monotony in the extensive use of a single color, as required by the shell method, it's important to vary textures. Texture both affects color and sets it off, owing to the play of light. Smooth surfaces reflect light, rougher ones partially absorb it. Thus the same color may appear lighter and brighter or darker and richer depending upon the nature of the material.

Light also sets up a fascinating and ever-changing pattern of shadows in textured material, varying its color according to the angle from which it is viewed. A room in which the carpet is a shag or twist, the walls either painted or covered with a textured material such as burlap, grasscloth or canvas, and the curtain fabrics of an open weave that allows light to come through can never have an uninteresting one-note look, even though a single color is repeated in all three of these major decorating elements.

Color can be too colorful

It isn't necessary to use your major color quite so extensively as the shell method prescribes. But for harmonious decorating, it *is* wise to make up your mind about what your major color is. New techniques and materials make possible a breathtaking range of effects undreamed of a few decades ago. Color is now imprisoned in filament yarns impervious to fading even in the strongest sunlight. Frames for furniture are molded of plastics in a rainbow of hues. Vinyl and other synthetics simulate natural materials, from leather to handwoven wool, in almost every color to be found in nature. It's easy to go overboard and use so many hues, in roughly equal amounts, that the decorating scheme lacks any one strong color note to which the others can be keyed.

Another mistake to avoid is the use of certain colors because they are currently fashionable. Fads, and your passion for them, will pass, but you may have to live with a carpet or a major piece of furniture for some time. Be careful too about choosing colors so brilliant that you tire of them easily. This doesn't mean that you must avoid vivid colors but only that you should use them with discretion. Two skillful examples of how to do this are shown on the opposite and the immediately following pages.

Another good way to use bold, brilliant colors is to reserve them for the smaller accents that give impact to a low-keyed color scheme.

Wood is also a color

Too often the characteristic hues of furniture woods are ignored in planning the color scheme of a room. Yet wood takes on depth and richness when set against an appropriate background, loses character when it is not. Here as elsewhere the rules of related or contrasting

One strong color, balanced by crisp white and black, creates a dramatic color scheme. Above, emerald green greets you as you enter the front door, continues in the adjacent living room shown on the opposite page. The border on the rug repeats the floral pattern covering the two chairs.

Use
your favorite color
in quantity

Vibrant red, accented by black
and softened by beige and white,
makes an exciting
yet easy-to-live-with room.
Here, the largest expanse of color
is provided by the room-size rug.
A color scheme of this type,
dependent on one major factor
for its strongest theme,
can be changed simply by retiring
the key piece to use elsewhere,
substituting a new color. A window
shade that matches the upholstery,
the striped fabric on the table,
are deft decorator touches.

Hot pink is cooled
by a white floral pattern
and deep-blue wall-to-wall
carpeting. Inexpensive
wicker headboard and a table
are painted to match
the fabric color.

color can be applied. Soft blues, blue-greens, and greens, for example, contrast with the warm tones of fine furniture and therefore flatter it. Yellow, beige, and coral are equally successful, but for the opposite reason—because they *are* related to wood tones. Greys, bright blues, and violets neither contrast with natural wood finishes nor relate well to them, and therefore form an unfriendly background. These colors are better used with painted furniture.

Practicality is still another consideration in the choice of color, particularly if your children are young. Some color-and-texture combinations—a thick, shaggy rug in earth tones, for example, or a multicolored tweed carpet—tend to disguise dust and dirt. Very light (or very dark) shades and smooth surfaces are more vulnerable. If you like the light, bright look, be sure to check for labels that identify soil-resistant finishes on fabrics and rugs, easily maintained hard floorings, and scrubbable paints and wall coverings.

Where to find a color scheme

Color schemes are all around you for the borrowing. An almost inexhaustible source is to be found in patterned fabrics, carpets, and wall coverings that combine two or more colors. Begin by selecting a printed or woven pattern that appeals to you. Then match the colors that appear in it in paint chips, fabric swatches, rug and wall covering samples. Play with these, adding or subtracting colors, varying the areas in which the colors are to be used, taking into account the basic rules of color (see pages 36–39), until you are confident that the scheme you have worked out is right.

Perhaps the original pattern you selected will be used as an upholstery or slipcover fabric. The wall color might then either match the background of the print or be painted a lighter value of that color, while the print's secondary color is borrowed for the floor covering. The color scheme of the room on the opposite page is derived in this manner; that on the following page is inspired by a handsome patterned screen.

Let the outside come indoors

A color scheme can also be derived, in exactly the same manner, from a favorite painting or print. And don't neglect the opportunity, if you are lucky enough to have a house with a view, to bring the outdoors inside. If you look out on trees, try wood-paneled walls, neutral colors in paints and floor coverings, nature's own browns and golds for upholstery and curtains. Then, like nature in bloom, splash in brilliant accents of color, but in small quantities.

If an expanse of water is a major part of your view, consider its brilliance and light-reflective qualities, which tend to wash out pale or neutral colors. Build your scheme around the colors of water itself—

Colors in the plaid upholstery fabric
inspired the scheme of this French provincial room.
The soft green of the rug is the lightest color
in the plaid; beams are painted its deepest blue.
Same fabric used for drapery covers farthest wall
and defines this area; other walls are painted off-white.
For accent, bright red is used above the beam shelf.

Yellow and deep blue are used strongly in this room,
with green, their intermediate color, underfoot
and covering two chairs. Entire scheme stems
from the hand-screened, floral-patterned folding screens

QUEEN MARGARET COLLEGE LIBRARY

used to divide the living from the dining areas.
The contemporary sofa and unexpected plastic cube tables,
the plastic shelves and lighting fixture in the dining area,
contrast pleasingly with the traditional furnishings.

green, blue, blue-green—with splashes of red-orange and yellow to warm it.

Whether you plan to decorate a room or a whole house from scratch or simply to add something new to an existing scheme, it is important to regard your home as a unit, particularly in terms of color. Most of today's houses and apartments are open in plan, with one room clearly visible from the next. In almost any house this is true of the living and dining rooms; both are almost always in view from the front door.

Let color flow through your house

Adjacent rooms that can be seen together should be coordinated in color, with variations in the intensity of the colors used, and in patterns and textures, to avoid monotony. A good example of such coordination in a high-keyed color scheme is shown on pages 44 and 45. In the living room (page 45), brilliant emerald green predominates against a white background; the second most important element is the bold print used on two chairs and as inspiration for the design of the rug border.

In the adjoining entrance hall (page 44), the print is eliminated; both floor and walls are white, and the green is repeated only in the stairway carpet and in plants that thrive in the strong daylight from the stairwell.

The adjacent dining room in this house (not pictured) is basically white, with touches of pink borrowed from the painting in the living room. In a unified color-flow plan, other rooms could play further variations on the original color scheme, with care taken to avoid the sudden shock produced by a completely unrelated mood. For instance, the kitchen might feature fruitwood cabinets, a white vinyl floor and white countertops; the accent colors could be pink, green, or yellow, all drawn from a patterned wall covering. The walls in a family room related to this kitchen might be wood-paneled, the upholstery white or yellow, with green accessories.

A color scheme of this type creates a pleasing harmony throughout the house without needless repetition of the same color. Children's rooms might sometimes be made an exception to the color-flow rule, to allow for strong individual preferences. But this kind of plan is so flexible that many variations can be worked into it without destroying the overall design. It should also be noted that the color theme could well begin with the exterior of the house. In the example used above, a green door and black shutters on a house painted white would immediately sound the key note.

In establishing an overall color scheme, you will want to carry at least one unifying color throughout your home. Sometimes this can be done with wall-to-wall carpeting and color-related hard flooring. Another way is to make use of the many coordinated patterns available in wall coverings. For example, for an entrance hall you might

Pattern can tie your colors together

If you feel
the colors in a room
have gotten
out of hand,
choose a cover fabric
that will
pull it all together.
Here, matching paint
on the door adds
further emphasis.
Whenever a pattern
is an important part
of your color scheme,
make sure it is
in proper balance.
Wing chair (not shown)
in same fabric
faces sofa seen here.

choose a wallpaper pattern that repeats the color of the living room's painted walls; for the dining room and other adjacent rooms, different but compatible patterns all related in color.

Color and period styles

For authentic period schemes, there are exact reproductions of old fabrics that establish the colors favored in particular eras. From the Renaissance on, revived interest in our classical heritage and the discoveries of archaeologists led to an appreciation of the sophisticated use of color made by earlier civilizations—Egyptian, Greek, Roman, Etruscan. The excavation, beginning in the mid-eighteenth century, of Pompeii, a Roman city buried by volcanic ash in 79 A.D., was especially influential. Oriental colors have also long affected western arts, particularly since Marco Polo's importation of Chinese silks and porcelains in the fourteenth century. More recently, African influences too have had a profound effect.

The colors associated with some period styles popular today are:

EARLY AMERICAN. The first settlers wove their own fabrics and dyed them with plant juices in strong, clear colors—red, blue and green.

LOUIS XV AND XVI. Walls of boiserie—carved wood—in natural tones

A collection of colorful pillows brightens a big square daybed in a family room that doubles as a guest room. In addition to being decorative, pillows make for more comfortable lounging or can be used to cushion the small tables, also handy for extra seating. Fixtures on the floor-to-ceiling pole lamp can be adjusted to direct light in any direction desired.

Soft green walls are a perfect foil for bright red
of the upholstery, creating a contrasting
color scheme accented with white. To change
the mood of the room, simply re-cover the cushions
in another color—perhaps blue or a deeper shade
of green—and paint the end table to match.
On the floor, brick-patterned vinyl tiles
and two-tone feature strips form a striking design.

or painted soft blue, grey, yellow, or eggshell were characteristic of these eighteenth-century French styles. Drapery, upholstery, and carpet colors were blue, rose, yellow, green, and beige. Furniture was pale grey, blue, yellow, or off-white, with gilding or striping.

FRENCH PROVINCIAL. Originally a less grand adaptation of the court styles of several periods, this encompasses a wide range of colors. Toile de jouy—a scenic pattern in red, blue, or green on a light background—and checks in red or blue are especially characteristic.

GEORGIAN. Covering 80 years of English styles, and including Chippendale, Hepplewhite, and Sheraton, this period most clearly influenced eighteenth-century America. Colors for most of the era were

Bathrooms too deserve careful color planning. Here, the plaid pattern on the cabinet doors is a jumping-off point; carpet, towels, accessories, are keyed to its colors. Lighting is also a particular interest, with built-in illumination over both lavatory areas (one on far side of room is reflected in the mirror).

Cool colors accentuate sleek, contemporary styling in a living room graced
with matching sofas separated by a long coffee table. Colors in carpet
combine blues and greens used throughout room. Pattern gains emphasis
by being limited to black and white, including ceiling with its stained beams.

An easy and effective way to create a color scheme is to let a painting
dictate it, then search for an important fabric to back it up. In this room,
the upholstery and drapery materials repeat the colors in the painting,
from clear yellow to hot red; rug and chair cushions hit a medium range

between the two. The green in the fabric is repeated on furniture frames.
Natural wood tones of the floor-to-ceiling paneling add to the warm effect.
Vinyl flooring extends throughout, with a rug defining the conversation area.
A game table and chairs at one end also serve for informal meals.

Color brings excitement
to an open-plan kitchen
and family room that combine
modern efficiency
with old-fashioned charm.
Bright red predominates;
the equally bright blue
of chairs in the dining area
is repeated on the far wall
of the family room. Cushions
of the white settle display
the same red pattern
used for chair cushions
and draperies in the kitchen.
Countertops are easy-care
plastic laminate; ceramic tile
is used for the range hood
and for the niche,
formed by storage cabinets,
for the Franklin stove.
Light fixture has a period air.

elegant and restrained: soft ivory, rose, green, and the shade known today as "Williamsburg blue" from the restoration of the colonial town of Williamsburg, Virginia. Later, in the Regency period, a dark "Pompeian red" became popular, as did rich shades of green, gold, and pink associated with the Orient.

VICTORIAN. Our immediate ancestors had a heavy hand with color, often using dark, almost muddy, brown or red backgrounds and strong reds, greens, and golds for drapery and upholstery. When the style is adapted for use today, the colors are usually lightened.

MODERN. The founders of this style, in the early part of the present century, emphasized off-white, beige, and other neutrals. Gradually this purist approach has been abandoned for one that uses brilliant colors at will, often against stark white backgrounds.

These color associations are useful not only for creating authentic period rooms but for imaginative mix-and-match schemes. Color can make a traditional room look contemporary, a contemporary room traditional.

pattern and texture

GIVE WALLS AND WALL COVERINGS, FLOORS, FURNITURE, AND FABRIC NEW DIMENSIONS

Except for color, nothing adds so much interest to a room as pattern and texture. In introducing both into your basic color scheme, you will begin to discover the endless possibilities to be found in fabrics and in floor and wall coverings. Assembling a really exciting combination of color, pattern, and texture can be as creatively satisfying as painting a picture.

Texture adds the dimension of depth

Although, technically, everything has texture, smooth surfaces lack the three-dimensional interest of rougher ones. An empty room with painted walls, a smooth floor, and an uncurtained expanse of glass at the windows is bland and dead-looking. Add a shaggy rug and pebbly-weave draperies and the room begins to come alive.

The shadow play that light sets up in textured materials, creating changing patterns and subtle nuances of color, is part of the magic. Another element is the pleasure that many textures, smooth or rough, give the sense of touch—a pleasure that is suggested just by looking at them. The cool, sleek feel of metal, the softness of satin, the rough touch of burlap contribute to the effect their use in a room produces.

The rule for texture is the same as that for color: Don't overdo it. Just as a room lacking in texture is bland, so one with an excess of textured materials, or one with too many different kinds, is distracting. What is needed is a delicate balance of smooth, pile, and rough textures, each one enhancing the others.

TEXT CONTINUED ON PAGE 66

In this dining room in a formal mood, a brick wall gives texture and a touch of piquancy. More texture, and contrasting pattern, are provided by the split bamboo used for the window blinds and the small folding screen. Nubbly rug, trimmed with fringe, effectively sets off the fine-grained wood of the table and chairs.

THE FEEL OF TEXTURE

Do you like to handle and to feel fabrics? Sometimes you can even tell whether you like them by the way they feel.

Building brick, gravel walls, and burlap curtains feel rough to the touch. Satin feels smooth— so does a painted window sill or a glass tumbler. Velvet feels soft —so does a kitten's fur; and moss feels soft and cool. "Hard as a rock" is a familiar expression. The skin of a peach feels fuzzy. Contrast the sharp scratchiness of steel wool or sandpaper with the cold, slick feel of metal.

Run your hand over your clothes, the top of the dining table, an upholstered chair, and a china plate. They all have a different feel because of texture.

THE LOOK OF TEXTURE

Sometimes you do "visual" touching. Some textures spell enjoyment to you and you are drawn to touch them; others indicate by their look that you will dislike them, and you avoid contact with them whenever possible. You know when you look at it that a thistle or a thorn will be prickly, or that steel wool or sandpaper will be rough. The rough look of some ceramic cups might make you decide that you do not want to drink from them.

You react in some way to every texture you see. So long as you do not touch them, some imitation textures—wallpaper that looks like cork, vinyl flooring that simulates brick—can create the effect of the real thing.

TEXTURE AFFECTS COLOR

Texture affects color as you see it. A shiny, smooth surface reflects light and the color appears clear and bright. Rough material absorbs or takes up some of the light and the color may appear deeper and duller. Velvet, because of its deep-cut pile, both absorbs and reflects light, so the color appears to be different in the folds of the fabric. If you put a piece of white satin and white muslin into the same kettle of dye and leave them the same length of time, the resulting color will appear to be somewhat different in each fabric because of their varying textures.

PATTERNS AND WEAVES PRODUCE TEXTURE

You will find a difference in texture within the same kind of material. Velvet made from cotton differs from that made from nylon in feel and appearance. Grasses differ—some are fine and soft, some are coarse to the touch. Plastered walls may be smooth or rough. Wood may be sanded satin smooth, but the grain pattern gives more texture to some types. Paper has many textures: the smooth, thin look of tissue; the coarse roughness of construction paper; the many variations in wallpaper; and all the different kinds of gift wrappings available today.

Small all-over patterns in upholstery or curtain fabrics lose their design detail and appear as a textured fabric. The design gives it the textured look. So pattern can contribute to the textured look of materials.

Examine the plain weave and fine thread of sheer, crisp organdy, the shaggy pile of turkish toweling, the deep pile of velvet, the scratchiness of coarsely woven wool, and the smooth finish of a percale sheet. Each of the many different weaves contributes to the final fabric texture, and each finds its own companions in other materials.

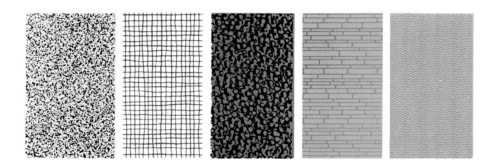

COMBINING TEXTURES

Rough textured objects seem to advance to take up more space, while smooth textured ones seem to recede. Experiment with textures when arranging accessories in your room. A small object with a very textured surface will generally balance a somewhat larger piece that has a smooth surface. The texture of wall covering or other background material will make a difference.

Experiment with textures in a room to find those that are suited to your furnishings. Smooth fabrics seem better suited to painted, delicately styled furniture. Heavier styles or coarse-grained woods may demand a sturdier fabric. Too much of the same texture can be monotonous.

Find out which textures you like to combine—smooth or coarse—formal or informal— whichever you prefer. Experiment to find which combinations you like. You may make changes as you become more sensitive to a variety of materials. You will probably acquire a taste for certain textures, just as you do for certain food flavors.

Texture can offer the same kind of exciting experiences you felt when working with color. The various textures can invite you to feel, to examine, and to explore many kinds of materials both indoors and out.

Here are some of the many possibilities to choose from in giving a room textural interest:

WALL COVERINGS. Among those with real texture you can feel are grass cloth, cork (in both tile and sheet form), bamboo, suede, burlap, and both fabrics and papers with velvetlike flocking. In addition, there is a vast variety of wallcloths and wallpapers, many of them vinyl-coated, that give the illusion of texture by simulating everything from silk to marble, including ticking, taffeta, damask, linen, monk's cloth, brick, and fieldstone. Some of them are so real-looking that you have to touch them to tell the difference. Yet they are far less expensive than the originals, and usually are easier to install (see page 224).

Then there is a whole category of prefinished wall paneling of solid wood; plywood, veneered or printed with wood graining; and printed hardboard. The latter comes not only with wood-grain patterns hard to distinguish from the real thing, but also in a number of colors and in designs resembling leather, marble, tile, and tapestry. Most paneling has a distinctive texture, either natural or manmade, and for easy maintenance is given a plastic coating by the manufacturer. Hardwood paneling is the most expensive, hardboard the least.

PAINT. There are some paints with texture incorporated into the mixture, to give a grainy or stuccolike effect. (Notice the wall in the room on page 68.) But once used, they are difficult to remove, nor can they be covered over to achieve a smooth surface. So be certain you really like the effect before you apply a textured paint.

MASONRY. Stone, brick, concrete, all have distinctive surfaces, often so three-dimensional that the play of light and shadow has a particularly handsome effect. The brick fireplace wall on the facing page, with its variegated texture accentuated by the mortar courses, is an example. Lightweight, flexible masonry panels, installed with nails and adhesive, are also available.

HARD FLOORING. You can use natural materials with tangible texture, such as wood, marble, brick, terrazzo, stone, or ceramic tile, or vinyl floorings that imitate these materials, including some patterns with surface indentations to increase the effect (see the next chapter).

FABRICS. Used for curtains, draperies, upholstery, slipcovers, floor coverings, bedspreads, and many other furnishings, these offer limitless variations in texture. The basic meaning of the word, in fact, is "something woven," a definition that also applies to most fabrics.

Linen comes in all textures from a heavy basket-weave to the finest gauze. *Cotton* ranges from silky percale to rugged corduroy. *Wool* is sometimes used for fine-textured casement cloths but is found more frequently in tapestry or frieze types of upholstery fabrics and in rugs and carpets. *Silk* has inspired the weaver to produce some of the most

Here the satisfying roughness of the reclaimed bricks
in the fireplace is counterpointed by a soft, shaggy rug,
metal-and-glass tables, and smooth upholstery fabrics;
repeated in the wood-paneled walls, time-worn
ceiling beams. Bricks, which vary in color
from pink to red, are laid in several different designs;
another pattern is represented in fabric on chairs.

delicate and beautiful fabrics: velvet, brocade, damask, taffeta, crêpe de chine, moiré, satin, and shantung.

Manmade fibers can be spun and woven to imitate the texture of almost any fabric made of natural fibers, as well as to create new effects. Often these synthetics are shrinkproof, fade-resistant, and have wrinkle-inhibiting permanent-press and/or soil-resistant finishes.

To take full advantage of the limitless color, pattern, and texture possibilities of fabric, use it in imaginative ways. Cover whole walls with it—stapled, tacked or pasted directly on the wall. Or frame shirred panels of fabric with wood molding. Dress up a table with a floor-length skirt; use fabric panels in folding screens, shutters, cupboard doors; paste motifs from a drapery fabric onto a window shade; cover the drawers or top of a chest to match a bedspread; hang a handsome rug on the wall.

Left: In a Spanish-style bedroom, stucco walls provide immediate textural interest; terra-cotta flooring adds color, pattern to the mix. Intricately wrought headboard (notice shadow design it forms on the wall), deeply carved chest supply more important pattern.

Right: Today's wallpapers, many of them vinyl-coated, offer an almost unlimited choice of colors and patterns.
1. Snakeskin print in warm, subdued tones. 2. Toile (short for toile de Jouy) is an 18th-century French scenic pattern. 3. Giant sunflowers, on a mustard background, set off a handsome dado and molding. 4. Bamboo pattern is used on a screen. Besides wallpaper, there are self-adhesive vinyl or vinyl-coated-fabric wall coverings.

Above: In this tiny dining room,
an appropriately small-patterned wallpaper
forms a striking foil for the scaled-down furniture.
(Most of today's wallpapers are washable; some,
especially those coated with vinyl, can be scrubbed.)
The ceramic-tile floor echoes the wallpaper motif;
a narrow shelf running around room at chair-rail height
provides display for accessories
without infringing on the room's limited space.
The round table is also a space saver.

Left: Larger dining room can take a bolder pattern;
white woodwork, overmantel, and window treatment
keep paper from being overwhelming. The floral figure,
reminiscent of crewel embroidery patterns,
enhances Colonial American furnishings, dominates
but does not clash with the traditional pattern
of the Oriental area rug.
Prepasted, pretrimmed wallpapers are easier to apply,
cost slightly more than the untreated kind. Design
and quality also affect price, with unusual
scenic effects and velvet-like flocked patterns
usually being in the higher price range.

TRIMMINGS. Fringes, guimpes, tassels, embroidery, and appliqué are useful for adding three-dimensional interest to a smooth fabric.

STRAW, CANE AND RUSH. Woven in a variety of ways, these contribute texture to chair seats, headboards, cabinet doors, mats, lampbases and shades, screens, baskets, trays.

The effect of texture may be formal or informal. Silk, damask, satin, taffeta, fine-grained woods, elaborately carved surfaces, are thought of as belonging in formal rooms; tweeds, muslin, chintz, brick, fieldstone, furs, in informal ones. Texture can also affect the dimensions of a room. In rugs, for example, a high or shaggy pile tends to "fill" the room from the bottom up, and makes a low ceiling seem even lower. Such a rug would be much more effective in a room with a pitched or vaulted ceiling.

Pattern creates interest

The presence of a design adds variety and excitement to any surface. Pattern is sometimes a byproduct of texture—as in a brick wall, for example, or a tiled floor—and this kind of pattern must be kept in

Left: Lavish use of a single pattern
creates a striking effect. Here an indigo-blue
toile fabric, perfect for complementing
the antique French furniture,
is used for bedspread, draperies, walls
(for wall application, coat wrong side of fabric
with adhesive; for best results, use spray type
that won't stain. Press fabric, panel by panel,
to wall). Checked fabric on cushion, also faithful
to period, repeats red of the carpet, wood tones.

Right: In this bedroom wood patterns dominate—
both the beautifully figured veneers used
for the traditionally styled furniture
and the soft blue tongue-and-groove wall paneling;
black-and-white striped chair adds crisp accent.
Note the subtle variations in texture, from wood
to shaggy carpeting to soft velvet of bedspread.
Wood paneling comes in many different finishes,
in narrow to wide to random-width planks
or without any joints. Investigate other types
of paneling too—cork, masonry, textured hardboard.

Color, pattern, and texture are used to unite
an adjoining living room (left) and family room (above).
White-brick fireplace has openings (actually back-to-back)
into both rooms; passthrough can be closed off
from either side by louvered doors. Brick, doors,
white ceramic tile on floor bounding chimney wall,
and brick-patterned vinyl tiles create a strong, simple design;
floral and plaid upholstery, arabesque wallpaper panels,
spark it. Warm red of rug, upholstery, unify all.

mind in planning a room. On the other hand, very small patterns lose their design when viewed from a distance; the effect is simply to give the material a textured look.

In general, though, when we speak of pattern we mean designs with a definite character that have been printed, woven, stamped, or otherwise produced in fabrics and in wall and floor coverings. To use them effectively, there are a few things to remember:

· The safest course is to avoid using more than one strong pattern in a room. However, some of the most striking effects are achieved by a combination of designs. And two important patterns will live very well together if they are related in design but different in scale. You might, for example, combine a pattern featuring a large rose design with a small allover rosebud print. Another possibility for the second (or a third) pattern would be a coordinated geometrical design such as a plaid, stripe or trellis motif. Both the wallpaper and the textile industry have developed many correlated and coordinated groups of patterns.

· For some wallpaper designs, there are matching drapery and upholstery fabrics, as in the French provincial bedroom on page 72. Notice how the large patterned areas on walls, bed, and windows are countered by the solid-color rug, curtains, and wood furniture.

· Similarly, a pattern in the rug or carpet often dictates plain walls and subdued designs in drapery or upholstery fabrics. Skillfully balanced by plain surfaces, however, patterned or Oriental rugs may be used with printed fabrics.

· Like color and texture, pattern can play tricks on your eyes. A wallpaper with a vertical design, by leading the eye upward, makes a ceiling look higher, while a strong horizontal motif seemingly lowers the ceiling's height. (Using wallpaper of any kind *on* the ceiling also makes it look lower.) A large pattern may seem out of scale in a small room, while in a large room, a small pattern tends to be overwhelmed. A great deal of pattern in a room seems to fill it up, reducing the need for furniture. (But be careful—too much pattern can make a small room look crowded.)

· Pattern can disguise architectural defects. If you have a hall or foyer cut up by many doors, cover walls *and* doors with an exciting pattern to give it a unified—and interesting—look. A small allover pattern is good for disguising patchy walls, jogs, and other blemishes.

· A bold, strongly colored, or splashy pattern is usually better confined to a fairly small area, where it will provide a center of interest. Used too lavishly, it can seem overpowering.

Here, one bold color and the traditional scenic design of the chair upholstery contribute to a country look, heightened by the subtle play of pattern and texture in the wood paneling, French provincial furniture, and vinyl tiled floor. Dramatic red accent is continued in the archway and accessories.

floors

LAY THE GROUNDWORK
FOR GOOD DECORATING

There are three ways to treat a floor: cover it entirely with carpet; cover it partially with a rug; or, if it is both handsome and functional, leave it bare. In most homes all three ways are represented, each meeting a particular need.

Basic flooring materials are called "hard surface," to distinguish them from rugs and carpet. They are especially appropriate where ease of maintenance is a major consideration. They may be either natural or man-made. Natural materials are difficult and expensive to install in an existing home, but are well worth considering if you are building or remodeling.

Natural hard-surface flooring

Among natural flooring materials in use for centuries are marble, clay tiles, flagstone, slate, brick, and, of course, wood.

MARBLE, once considered a luxury, is now available in a thinner gauge that is less expensive and easier to install. It is especially suitable for small areas, such as a foyer or bathroom. Even for larger rooms—a living or dining room—the cost is not out of line if measured against that of a rug or carpet, not needed on a handsome marble floor. Marble comes in marvelous colors, may be used to achieve either a formal or informal effect, and needs only an occasional washing to maintain its pristine appearance.

FLAGSTONE, SLATE, AND BRICK produce an informal or country look (see the rooms on pages 82–83 and 90–91). The textural effect is pleasant and the care needed minimal. These materials are all porous

Brick-like vinyl tiles, laid in a herringbone design, make a handsome and practical floor for a foyer and dining room, creating—with houseplants, green-and-white color scheme, bamboo-patterned walls— a fresh-as-a-garden air. Fabric-paneled folding doors provide privacy while letting light in.

78

In this living room,
clearly visible
from the front door,
the tortoise-hued carpet
echoes the color
of the ceramic tiles
in the entrance hall.
Ceramic lamps
light the few steps down
to the living room; wood molding,
étagère, contribute
to the warm color scheme.

and should be treated with a sealer to keep stains from penetrating. Once so treated, only an occasional sweeping or scrubbing is necessary.

TERRA COTTA AND CERAMIC-GLAZED TILE offer a wide range of choices. Both have a long history of use, particularly in countries bordering the Mediterranean and in the Middle East. Unglazed terra-cotta quarry tile comes in natural earth tones and is used in informal settings. More formal effects can be achieved with glazed and ornamented ceramic tile, available in a variety of colors and patterns.

WOOD FLOORING is of two basic types. Most familiar is the kind in which the planks all run in the same direction and are of a standard width, as in the floor on the opposite page. Widths available range from very narrow to the broad ones used in early colonial houses.

Parquet, or patterned flooring, the most formal in effect, is created by cutting narrow strips of wood into short lengths, forming them into squares in checkerboard, herringbone or other patterns, and joining the squares to achieve a floor of the desired area. The design thus produced may be heightened by alternating the direction of the grain in the squares. Parquet floors (for an example, see page 229) are handsome enough to eliminate the need for a rug.

Both standard and parquet flooring may be stained to darken the wood, or bleached and given a color stain to create an exotic effect.

Because wood is porous, a new hardwood floor should be sealed by varnish or some other means. To protect a floor against soil and scratching, wax is needed. This may be a polishing wax or the newer self-polishing type made especially for wood floors. (If you plan to color an old floor, be sure to sand it first to remove the wax and varnish; otherwise the stain will not penetrate.)

CONCRETE—after sanding, buffing, sealing and waxing—makes an admirable flooring material. It is possible to add color to the mix before it is put down.

Manmade hard-surface flooring

Man-made floorings come in a dazzling variety of patterns and colors. In addition, they are resilient underfoot and easy to maintain.

Which material should you choose? All those listed below will last

Here, narrow wooden boards, stained and waxed, form an easily maintained dining-room floor that is too handsome to cover up. Notice how the vertical blinds, painting, clock, act as counterpoint to the horizontal feeling of the furniture.

*Soften
a hard-surface floor
with a shaggy rug*

Natural flagstone is used
throughout the first floor
of this open-plan house;
a sealer, applied after stone
is laid, makes it impervious
to spills. For warmth, softness,
a brilliantly colored shaggy rug
outlines the conversation area,
contrasts with the subtle color
and pattern of the floor beneath.
In dining area at left,
rollup matchstick blinds
control glare
while letting light pour in
through the upper portion
of the floor-to-ceiling windows.

for years if they are properly installed and cared for. Therefore, durability is not as important a concern as it is when you buy a rug or carpet. That doesn't mean you can buy for good looks alone. For any area where there's a great coming and going—of children, guests, deliverymen, pets, et cetera—look for medium rather than very light or dark colors, and for attractive but fairly "busy" patterns that camouflage footmarks, spills, and splashes. And think twice about rough-surfaced or deeply indented materials. No matter how appealing, they may present washing and waxing problems. (However, many of the newer patterns require no waxing—only washing.

Another factor to consider is where the flooring will be installed. Some materials cannot be used in basements ("below grade") or on the ground floor ("on grade") of basementless houses, because of the moisture to which they would be exposed. Price and ease of installation are other considerations. With some materials, it is possible to save money by installing the floor yourself.

VINYL. The hard-surface material most in demand today is the newest on the scene—vinyl, a creation of chemistry. It comes in sheet form and in tiles. In both types, a vast number of patterns, both textured and smooth, are available, some simulating natural materials—wood, marble, flagstone, brick, and a host of others. Or you can create your own designs by mixing and matching patterns and colors.

Also available are asphalt tile, rubber tile, vinyl-coated cork tile, and the still popular old standby, linoleum. Here is a rundown:

Sheet vinyl comes in 6-foot widths; some patterns are also available in 9- and even 12-foot widths, to reduce or eliminate the need for seams. (The fewer the seams, the easier the care.) In *inlaid vinyl* the pattern goes all the way through to the backing, but is limited to variations of a chip design, and the surface is smooth. In *rotogravure* and *embossed vinyl*, the sky's the limit in both pattern and texture, but the surface layer of vinyl is relatively thin. There is also *cushioned vinyl*, which has a backing of spongy foam material that means extra comfort in walking, quieter steps, and a warmer floor.

Some sheet vinyls can be used on or below grade; some can't. Check with your dealer when you buy.

Solid vinyl tile (like the other tiles listed below) comes in 9-inch and 12-inch squares. It can be used in any location.

Vinyl-coated cork tile has many of the advantages of natural cork—quiet, beauty, and comfort underfoot. It should not be used below or on grade, or in kitchens or bathrooms.

Kitchen floor with a custom look like this one
is easily attained with the help of "feature strips,"
sold by the yard as is sheet flooring
(here a subtly patterned linoleum). Decorator cabinets
can be copied by applying wood molding, brass hardware,
to stock models; cafe curtains hang from painted rods.

Vinyl asbestos tile is cheaper than solid vinyl, resists stains and wears well. Some types are self-adhering—to install, just peel off the backing and press the tile into place. Vinyl asbestos tile can be used anywhere.

LINOLEUM, available in sheet form, is durable, long-wearing and easy to clean. Embossed patterns lend textural interest. However, linoleum should not be used below or on grade.

RUBBER TILE is comfortable and quiet, but requires consistent waxing (use only self-polishing or water-based polishing wax) to maintain its appearance. Rubber tile can be installed anywhere.

ASPHALT TILE is low in cost but susceptible to dents and stains. Some types are grease-resistant. Use only self-polishing wax or water-based polishing wax, and avoid the use of solvents. Asphalt tile can be installed in any location.

Soft-surface flooring—carpets

Soft-surface flooring is the trade term for all kinds of rugs and carpets. In general, the word *carpet* refers to wall-to-wall carpeting, *rug* to a floor covering of lesser extent. Room-size rugs cover most of the floor, coming to within a few inches of the baseboard. Area rugs, as the name implies, are smaller.

Carpet is woven on broadlooms in widths of nine, twelve, fifteen, and eighteen feet. (Hence "broadloom carpeting"—a term that refers simply to width, not quality.) If the floor you want to cover has one dimension·that matches a broadloom width, you can have a seamless wall-to-wall carpet. Most rooms are not so conveniently sized, and some seaming is almost always necessary.

Wall-to-wall carpeting looks and feels luxurious, makes a room seem larger, cuts down noise, and makes furniture arrangements more flexible. It is also more expensive, owing to the greater area covered and the installation charge. It *can* be taken up and relaid if you move, but there is inevitably some waste involved. And it cannot be turned around (to vary wear) or sent out for cleaning as rugs can.

Carpets come in a luscious array of colors—scarlet, melon, canary, straw, jade, moss gold, frosty pearl, citron, apricot, shocking pink, sable, ginger, bayberry, tangerine, silver-blue—and so on, through hundreds and hundreds of hues. And if even those don't satisfy you, some manufacturers keep a supply of "white goods" on hand to be dyed to your specifications.

The rug or carpet is a key factor in a room's color scheme and

In an inviting contemporary living room,
shaggy wall-to-wall carpeting underscores the promise
of casual comfort and ease
offered by the clean-lined upholstered furniture.
The factory-finished wood paneling on the walls
is an effective backdrop for the picture grouping.

*Major types
of carpet construction*

Cut pile

Single-level loop

High-and-low loop

should be chosen with care. Another consideration is practicality. In the beige family, rose-beiges tend to change more, in time, from their original color than yellow-beiges do—soil tends to "grey" the rose hue. White and pale tints of any color show soil the most, medium values (shades that are neither too light nor too dark) the least. Two-tone mixtures and tweeds are good soil-concealers too. Further camouflage is possible with all-over patterns. The same general rules hold for disguising traffic or wear lanes, with the addition that a low, dense pile is more efficient at hiding indentations than a high, loose one.

There is a wide choice of texture and pattern in carpeting. Formal effects can be achieved with plush, grospoint, overall or multicolored designs, and carpets with carved or sculptured pile. Tweedy or heathery mixtures, shags, and informal printed designs create a more casual mood. When considering pattern and texture in rugs and carpets, the dimensions of the room should also be kept in mind, for the reasons explained on page 76. Remember too that a bold pattern on the floor may limit your pattern choices in the rest of the room.

Which texture is best?

There *is* no best texture. Each one has different characteristics, which affect both the look of the carpet and how it will behave. Which one is best for you will depend on the combination you want. Densely packed, short-to-medium piles can take the most wear.

Single-level-loop carpeting changes least in appearance when given hard wear. Tight, low loops wear best.

High-low loop creates a patterned effect with two or more levels and is also quite durable.

Random-sheared has a sculptured look, with some low-level loops and some higher, sheared pile. Unless pile density is thick, the pattern tends to flatten out under traffic.

Tip-sheared is similar to random-sheared, but the loops and the cut pile are on the same level. These two sheared textures will not show lint or traffic lanes as much as all-cut pile.

Velvet (or plush), which is all-cut pile, always shows a characteristic shading from traffic; the denser the pile, the less shading.

Shag has a ¾- to 2-inch pile, which is quick to show indentations from traffic and tends to mat in high-traffic areas.

Twist is made with very tightly twisted yarn, which creates an irregular surface. It is quite durable.

Which fiber is best?

Again, the answer depends on what you want in terms of looks, ease of cleaning, resiliency, and price, among other factors.

Wool fibers have outstanding resiliency; thus wool carpets have

In a traditional living room,
a room-size rug in cool blue
both takes its color from
and creates a soothing contrast to
the exuberant and brightly colored
floral design of the upholstery
and draperies. Green of the walls
picks out another color in the print;
mahogany wood tones still another.
The dropfront Chippendale desk
is an antique; other furnishings
are contemporary copies
of Colonial American styles.

excellent crush resistance and shed soil easily. Today, most wool and wool-blend carpets have been mothproofed by the manufacturer.

Man-made fibers are moth- and mildew-resistant by virtue of their composition. Among them:

Acrylic fibers look the most like wool and perform well. Crush resistance is good when the carpet is well constructed and has a dense pile. Some trade names: Acrilan, Creslan, Orlon 33, Zefkrome. Acrylic-modacrylic blends are often used. The modacrylic fibers are Dynel and Verel.

Nylon fibers have excellent abrasion resistance; they also have good strength and resiliency. Pilling and snagging can be a problem with loose-loop textures. Some trade names: Caprolan, 501 Nylon, Cumuloft, Enkaloft. Anso, Antron, Cadon, Enkalure have superior soil resistance.

Polyester fibers have very good resiliency and are noted for the brilliance of their color. Some trade names: Avlin, Dacron, Encron, Fortrel, Kodel, Tough-Stuff, Trevira.

Polypropylene fibers have superior resistance to stains but tend to crush more easily than other fibers. Some trade names: Herculon, Marvess, Polyloom, Vectra.

Nylon/polyester fiber gives a soft, silky look, yet is durable. Trade name: Source.

How does price compare?

Generally speaking, wool carpets are highest in price, followed by polyester and acrylic, then by nylon and polypropylene. Within each fiber category there is also a range of price—and quality. The more yarn packed into a carpet, the better the carpet. If the pile is skimpy and you can see a lot of backing, don't buy the carpet. Durability depends more on density than on texture or fiber content—or how the carpet is made (tufted or woven).

Every carpet and rug should have good padding underneath, to absorb the crush of wear and thus lengthen the carpet's life, to act as a sound absorber, and to provide buoyancy and comfort underfoot. The most luxurious-feeling padding is made of sponge or foam rubber. Urethane foam also is buoyant and costs less. The flatter all-hair and hair-and-jute pads also do a good job; they are the least costly.

In addition to regular carpeting, there are some special types:

INDOOR-OUTDOOR CARPETING.   This represents a special type of floor covering. It will live up to its name and be useful on a patio as well as in a kitchen or bathroom only if *all* the materials used in it are impervious to weather. If either the surface or the backing absorbs moisture, mildew and bad odor will develop. Read the label to make sure the surface is of such fibers as solution-dyed polypropylene or acrylic, with polypropylene or a special moisture-proof rubber backing.

KITCHEN CARPETS.   Although impractical in a household with very young children or pets, where a carpet would need constant attention to banish the multitude of stains and crumbs, in other homes kitchen carpeting can cut down on noise, provide a cushion underfoot and reduce glass and dish breakage. A moisture-proof indoor-outdoor carpet can be used in the kitchen. Also available are carpets designed specifically for kitchens. A good choice is a smooth-surfaced, single-level, low-loop nylon or polypropylene carpet with rubber backing.

Early American character of this room is underlined
by the brick floor, with a braided oval rug
whose colors repeat the variegated tones of the brick
to define the conversation area. (Brick-patterned
vinyl flooring can create much the same effect.)
Note how the modern Lawson sofa fits into the scheme.

On a smooth low-pile carpet, spills and crumbs stay on the surface and can be sponged or vacuumed away with ease.

Soft-surface floor covering—rugs

Rugs may be preferable to wall-to-wall carpeting if your basic flooring is attractive, if you move frequently, or if you like the convenience of being able to send your floor coverings out to be cleaned. A rug can also be turned to distribute the wear, thus prolonging its life. And rugs are available in marvelous patterns.

Many room-size rugs are simply cut from broadloom carpeting. Others are woven in standard sizes, 6' x 9', 8' x 10' and 9' x 12' being the most common. In the case of patterned rugs, each is designed, in scale, to the chosen size. Shapes are usually rectangular or oval, and borders or decorative fringe are often used.

Area rugs may be round, square, octagonal, oval, free-form, or almost any shape you can think of. Such a rug is usually chosen to define and coordinate a furniture grouping, as in a conversation area, around a fireplace, or in an area meant for dining. Because area rugs are meant to call attention to themselves, and because they are not big enough to dominate the room, designers can give free rein to their imagination. Some area rugs are so outstanding in design and color that they approximate a work of art. Often they are treated as just that, and hung on the wall.

Some special types among room-size and area rugs:

ORIENTAL RUGS were originally woven and knotted by hand and colored with vegetable dyes. Today, in the East, some are still handmade, but aniline dyes are used. Many more are made by machine, but continue the beautiful traditional designs and colors.

The designs are named for the tribe or country of origin, and each has a distinctive pattern, color, and texture. Kashan, Kirman, and Sarouk rugs are Persian in origin; soft in color, they feature floral, bird, and animal designs. Turkish rugs are brighter, with floral and geometric figures; among them are Kurdistan, Saraband, and Mozul. Turkestan rugs (which originated in an area now divided between China and Russia) are mainly red and brown with geometric patterns.

An Oriental rug is appropriate in either a traditional or contemporary setting. By virtue of its intricate pattern and handsome colors, it can establish an entire color scheme or design theme; examples are shown on pages 11 and 70. Most Orientals are made of wool and are extremely durable.

A modern version
of an antique Aubusson rug
adds superb pattern
in the traditional manner
to an eclectically furnished room
with a Directoire feeling.

In a sophisticated dining room, a room-size rug
with a contemporary pattern (a practical one too,
since it disguises all but the most disastrous spills)
is combined with traditionally styled furniture.
Chairbacks match the fabric covering of the buffet,
louvered shutters cover one whole wall, flank window.

SCANDINAVIAN OR RYA RUGS, usually made of wool or flax, gained popularity with the emergence of modern as a style in furnishings. Sweden and Denmark, early exponents of contemporary design, pioneered in the creation of shaggy, textured rugs, richly colored and abstract in design, to complement their clean-lined furniture. Rugs of this type create great decorative interest in any room.

LOWER-PRICE RUGS AND CARPETS. Here you will find self-adhesive carpet squares complete with under padding; you simply peel off the backing and press the square against the floor. Also in the lower price range: grass and sisal squares and matting, varicolored cotton rag rugs, braided rugs, and cotton shags. Cotton soils more readily than most other fibers and is best used in smaller sizes that may be washed.

When you shop for either hard- or soft-surface floor coverings, consider color first, then texture and pattern, to complement the look and feeling of the room you have in mind. Then be sure to get the quality you need, remembering that heavily trafficked areas call for better-grade coverings to stand up to the wear.

There are several types of rugs you can make yourself (see *Good Housekeeping New Complete Book of Needlecraft*):

HAND-HOOKED RUGS employ a tool that looks like a heavy crochet hook with a thick wooden handle. The hook, threaded with strips of fabric, is punched through the right side of the backing (burlap, monk's cloth or warp cloth), and the fabric pulled up from the wrong side to form a loop. Hooking may also be done from the wrong side.

BRAIDED RUGS are best made of wool, cotton, silk, or nylon fabric strips. The strips should be uniform in width and dimension. Usually three are used to form a braid, though up to eight strips are possible (you can buy a little gadget to speed up the braiding process). Lengths of finished braid are then laced together by hand to form the rug. The most common shapes are round, beginning with a circle of braid in the center, and oval, starting from an elongated loop of braid. Braided rugs are especially appropriate in early American rooms.

NEEDLEPOINT AND CROSS-STITCH RUGS are embroidered, using a good grade of yarn, on a special mesh canvas. Needlepoint canvases can be bought with the design already filled in, leaving the background to be done, or stamped with pattern and appropriate colors.

CROCHETED RUGS may be made of heavy yarn or bias-cut strips of fabric. A variety of stitches may be used to create designs.

Here, hot colors, in a free-form abstract pattern, cover the floor and establish the scheme for the whole room. Rug colors are repeated in the woolen draperies; the upholstery picks up the red, the pillows the violet tones. Painting over the fireplace combines the two.

furniture

IS FOR COMFORT
AND FOR STYLE

More than anything else, furniture establishes a room's style. In addition it may represent your biggest decorating expenditure. When you buy a sofa, or a dining room table and chairs, it is fairly certain you will be living with them for some time.

That is a good reason to choose carefully, but not to worry about your choice. Three factors are involved in furniture selection: style, comfort, and quality. Knowing what is involved in each of these takes the fear out of shopping.

Traditional versus modern design

There has never been a greater choice in furniture styles than today. New techniques combining machine and hand labor have made possible a vast selection, in both contemporary designs and period styles. On pages 98 through 100 you will find a description of styles that are still represented today—either in exact reproductions or in adaptations that retain a great deal of the original feeling. Because chair design is most typical of a given style, chairs have been chosen as illustrations. (If you want to go further into the subject, you'll find suggestions for study in Books for Further Reading, on page 243.)

The old styles are still strong because most women prefer a traditional feeling in their homes. Fortunately, that does not mean sacrificing comfort to appearance. New designs for solving old problems, such as dual-purpose sofas and ingenious storage units, are equally

TEXT CONTINUED ON PAGE 102

Simple and enduring style of Early American
is a perennial favorite. Here, modern versions
of a classic American Windsor chair, Queen Anne
wing chair, Hitchcock side chair, and country spice chest
blend perfectly with an antique hutch cupboard.
Plaid pattern on the sofa is repeated in the valance.

CHART OF FURNITURE STYLES

ITALIAN RENAISSANCE,
c. 1675

VENETIAN, C. 1750

EARLY ENGLISH, C. 1675

QUEEN ANNE, C. 1720

LOUIS XIV, C. 1700

LOUIS XV, C. 1750

LOUIS XV, C. 1750

LOUIS XVI, C. 1780

ITALIAN, dating back to the Renaissance (1400–1600). Large in scale and made of oak or walnut, heavily carved and paneled. Today's versions are smaller, to fit modern houses. Credenzas, trestle tables, and X-base chairs are typical of the early style. During the seventeenth and eighteenth centuries, the carving became more elaborate, intricate inlaid designs in wood or metal were often featured, and painted, gesso, and gilt finishes were widely used.

SPANISH (1500–1700). Quite similar to Italian styles of the same period but with a strong Moorish influence. Furniture was less delicately made and more deeply carved. Elaborate wrought-iron bases and hardware, metal studding for decoration, are characteristic. Tooled leather was often used for chair seats.

EARLY ENGLISH, Tudor and Jacobean periods (1500–1650). Furniture was ponderously made of carved oak with thickly turned legs, square shapes in chests and chairs. Caning appeared during the reign of William and Mary (1689–1702); designs also became lighter and more graceful, hardware more delicate.

QUEEN ANNE (1702–1714). This period marked the introduction of the cabriole leg and padded fabric upholstery. Pieces were delicately curved, lighter in scale, and simpler in design.

FRENCH COURT STYLES (1610–1793). Developed during the reigns of four Louis, these are the most formal and elegant of all. Chief characteristics of the various styles are: *Louis XIII*, straight lines, square shapes, elaborate carving; *Louis XIV*, silhouettes still straight and square but massive and baroque, with even more elaborate carving, and painted or gilded finishes; *Louis XV*, curving rather than square lines, cabriole legs; carving, metal inlay, and painted vignettes used for decoration; smaller in scale, far more luxurious and ornate; *Louis XVI*, simpler and more classic in styling, straight lines with carved classic motifs or painted decoration.

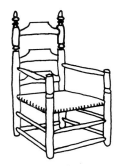

RLY AMERICAN, C. 1675

EARLY AMERICAN,
C. 1750

FRENCH PROVINCIAL. A simpler version of ornate court styles of several periods. Usually of various fruitwoods, often carved or painted.

ENCH PROVINCIAL, C. 1775

GEORGIAN, or EIGHTEENTH-CENTURY ENGLISH (1714–1795). For the first time, styles begin to be named for their designers. The most famous names are Chippendale, Hepplewhite, Sheraton, the Adam brothers. All worked during the latter part of the Georgian period. *Chippendale* styles borrowed heavily from earlier English furniture, from ornate French court designs, and from Chinese styles, to all of which Chippendale gave his own rococo interpretation. The wood used was almost always mahogany, then newly imported, with decorative carvings in a variety of classical motifs; chair seats were often richly upholstered. Books of Chippendale's designs were the inspiration for other cabinetmakers in England and in the American colonies. *Sheraton* designs were simpler, often with slender fluted legs and graceful flowing lines. Sheraton used rosewood and satinwood as well as mahogany, and carving, inlay, marquetry, or painted finishes for decoration. Upholstery fabrics were often of damask, striped satin. Sheraton's design books were also widely used by cabinetmakers in England and abroad. *Hepplewhite* furniture was even more restrained than Sheraton, with extremely graceful and simple lines. Legs were usually square and tapered, with spade feet; chair backs carved in an open pattern such as a shield, an oval, or interlaced hearts.

AMERICAN SHERATON,
C. 1795

HEPPLEWHITE, C. 1780

EARLY AMERICAN (1620–1720). Encompasses the early Pilgrim styles. Furniture was simple, strictly utilitarian and sometimes quite primitive; it was often homemade of native woods. Banister- and ladder-back chairs, hutch cupboards, trestle and butterfly tables, hooded cradles, are typical.

AMERICAN SHERATON,
C. 1790

CHINESE CHIPPENDALE,
C. 1765

COLONIAL AMERICAN (1720–1776). As the colonies prospered, they began to import European furniture; also, skilled craftsmen, attracted by a wealthy new market, immigrated to them. Furniture produced in the colonies was usually inspired by styles favored in the mother country: New York (then New Amsterdam) was Dutch-oriented; New England preferred English styles. Spanish styles flourished in Florida and the southwest, German in Pennsylvania, and both English and French in the southern colonies. There was, however, little slavish copying; instead, local tastes and needs were considered. Among distinctive styles, the Amercan version of the English Windsor chair was universally popular. It was usually made by the local wheelmaker; chair spindles were merely a more delicate version of wagon-wheel spokes.

PHILADELPHIA CHIPPENDALE,
C. 1770

HEPPLEWHITE, C. 1790

AMERICAN HEPPLEWHITE, C. 1795

FRENCH EMPIRE, C. 1810

AMERICAN EMPIRE, C. 1810

DUNCAN PHYFE, C. 1810

ENGLISH REGENCY, C. 18

AMERICAN VICTORIAN
C. 1860

CLASSIC MODERN, 19

DANISH MODERN, 194

CHART OF FURNITURE STYLES

FRENCH EMPIRE (1804–1815). This style originated with Napoleon's France and reflects his imperial ambitions. It is classic and simple in design, with eagles, wreaths, and other motifs reminiscent of the Roman Empire.

AMERICAN EMPIRE, also known as FEDERAL (1795–1830). Marks a gradual transition from eighteenth-century styles to a heavier design concept. Toward the end of the period, furniture was generally more massive, with thick and deeply carved legs. *Duncan Phyfe,* most famous of American cabinetmakers, worked during the latter part of this period, producing graceful and distinctive pieces. The lyre was his favorite motif, appearing on chair backs or on carved supports for tables. He used mahogany almost exclusively, beautifully and delicately carved in swags, wheat sheaves, fluting, oak leaves, and other motifs. Furniture legs were often formed in the shape of animal feet and usually were brass-tipped.

BIEDERMEIER (1800–1850). Developed in Germany as a revolt against the rococo and baroque styles that preceded it. Simple lines, with a sophisticated approach to the use of different woods, are characteristic.

ENGLISH REGENCY (1780–1830). Refers to the period in which George, Prince of Wales (later Prince Regent and later still George IV) influenced the decorative arts. It was a period of great opulence, with styles inspired by French Empire and by classical, Chinese, and Egyptian influences. Furniture was light and graceful, fabrics rich; woods used were mahogany, satinwood, and rosewood.

VICTORIAN (1837–1901). Rosewood was much favored for heavy, ornately carved furniture, often with floral motifs and inlays of mother-of-pearl or of brass. Marble-topped pedestal tables were popular. Today's adaptations are more restrained, often better-looking than the originals.

MODERN (1919–   ). Based on the concept that form follows function, a spare approach to design that calls for excellent materials used with a keen understanding of their intrinsic esthetic value. Modern employs full and handsome use of contemporary materials as well as methods of molding and forming not available to traditional designs.

ENGLISH REGENCY, C. 1810

Modern styling takes maximum advantage
of the inherent beauty of materials. The simple lines
of the sofa in this family room are complemented
by a handsomely striped and textured fabric; rosewood
is molded to create the ottoman; natural-color caning
accents the graceful curves of the black-framed chair.
Lamps, though dissimilar, are equally important;
weight of the geometrically decorated chest
balances the larger lamp table. Tile is used
to cover one wall, knotty elm paneling the others.

popular. Moreover, almost everyone these days plays the rewarding game of mix and match.

If you love a period style just the way it is, and if it fits in with your family's way of life, by all means adopt it. You can do so entirely with antiques, if you can afford them, as in the charming room on page 11; with reproductions or adaptations (see pages 24–25), or with a mixture of the old and the new, as shown on page 97. On the other hand, it's also fun to mix styles, either because they're so similar that they live well together, or for the exactly opposite reason—because the contrast provides excitement. The one rule is to choose pieces with the same feeling—formal or informal, striking or serene. By virtue of its simple lines, the sofa from the completely contemporary room on page 103 could be used with many traditional styles.

You'll find good design and bad in both modern and period furniture. Exact reproductions of period styles are exempt from this generalization because they are copied from the best models. If you prefer adaptations—and many people do, finding them better suited to their needs—or if you are in love with contemporary designs, look first for harmonious proportions. Avoid furniture in which fussy detail or a gaudy finish tries to disguise bad design.

Upholstered furniture provides comfort

In choosing upholstered furniture, comfort should come first, both for practical reasons and because the style of a room is usually established not by the upholstery pieces but by the more distinctive wood furniture. Completely upholstered furniture is the most versatile because its feeling is largely determined by the fabric chosen to cover it. Upholstered pieces in which the frame is exposed are less adaptable should you later decide to change the room's style or to slipcover the furniture.

A sofa and one or two upholstered chairs form the nucleus of a living-room arrangement. Because they represent so important an investment, think well ahead when you buy. If you are furnishing your first house or apartment, a sofa bed might be a good choice. Later it could be used in a family room, converting it, on a moment's notice, to a guest room. Size is an important consideration too. An average-length sofa will fit in any living room, but a king-size piece might be difficult to place should you move.

You might also consider, instead of a standard sofa, a curved sectional type, or two smaller sofas at right angles to each other, or a sofa and a love seat, or a pair of love seats. These all make for flexibility in arranging conversation groupings. Upholstered chairs may be of the same style as the sofa, but often they are more interesting if they are not. The fabrics used to cover them may also differ in color and pattern or texture.

When shopping for upholstered furniture, both you and your husband should try out each potential purchase. Take your time; try

Modern coffee table and cube that may be used either as a table
or a stool live comfortably with the lamp table and wood-framed chair,
adaptations of 19th-century pieces. Glen-plaid suiting covers the sofa.

it several times and sit in it for a while. There is an amazing difference between personal needs for comfort. Although you may have to compromise on a sofa if you can't find one that is right for both of you, each of you should have a chair that exactly meets your needs. The critical dimensions are seat height and depth. Your feet should reach the floor while your back easily touches the chair back.

What's inside is important

You can't, of course, *see* the inner construction of an upholstered piece. But you can still be sure of what you are getting, if you buy from a reliable store and know what questions to ask the salesman. Study the diagrams on page 106 to identify the different types of construction. Then, when you shop, ask in which category the piece you are considering belongs.

Look too for tags and labels that identify the cushioning and other materials used. Filling materials, such as polyester fiberfill, are used to give durable shape to upholstered furniture. In lower-priced pieces, filling is kept to a minimum or eliminated. Padding (felted cotton, foam) is used over the filling, in better furniture, to give final shape and surface resilience. In cheaper lines, the filling and the padding may be one and the same thing.

Cushion fillings, in descending order of quality are: spring cores covered with insulation and padding, often foam; latex foam; layered urethane foam; and last, plain urethane foam. For soft seat and back cushions (the kind you sink into—and have to plump up often) foam cores encased in fine polyester fiberfill have largely replaced natural down—still available on special orders.

Unless you buy a floor sample, you'll almost always have a wide choice of covering fabric. (Since this is a custom order, allow delivery time of from four weeks to three months.) Naturally you'll first look for the color, pattern, and texture you want. But before you buy, there are several other things to think about.

Choose fabrics carefully

Upholstery fabrics are usually arranged in grades according to price, from A (the lowest-priced grade) through B, C, D, E, and so on. An average sofa requires between 12 and 14 yards of upholstery fabric, so the difference between a $4-a-yard fabric and a $12 one can add a

Bold pattern and one singing color give a family room
the new-as-today look. The same striking fabric
used on the loveseat covers the cushions
of the two chairs (foreground) ; the chair frames
are sheathed in supremely functional black plastic.
Amusing lime-slice tables, accessories, complete theme.

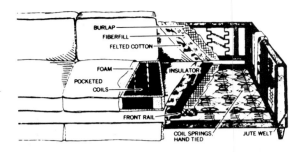

Traditional method of construction offers top comfort, costs more because of extra attention to detail— as hand-tied coil springs, lateral coil supports for back springs, taut burlap reinforced with steel on arms.

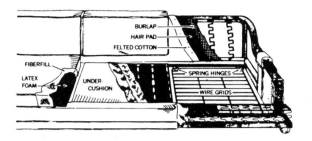

Unique mattress-type of construction is found in a medium- to high-price line of upholstered furniture with a base of wire grids; individual under-cushions are constructed like the finest bed mattresses.

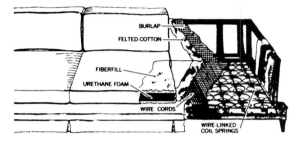

Modern version of traditional construction is used for medium-priced sofas. Base of wire-linked coil springs covered with burlap-backed wire cords. Felted cotton pads base and fiberboard arms; cushions are urethane foam.

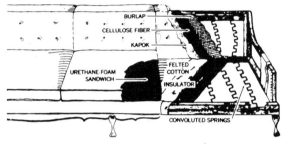

Firm comfort at less cost with base of convoluted springs covered with cellulose fiber and padded with felted cotton; rigid fiberboard arms are foam padded. Cushions are stiff foam sandwiched between two layers of softer foam.

hundred dollars or more to the price. Yet the most expensive fabric is not necessarily the most durable. Very often tough cottons and synthetics are available in the lower-price range, while some higher-priced materials are delicate and vulnerable. Among the best choices for durability are nubby-textured tweeds and tightly woven tapestries and damasks. Hard-surface wools are a good bet, as are closely woven cottons, nylon blends, and polypropylenes. (Check tags and labels for fiber content.)

If you're choosing a quilted fabric, watch for close, secure stitching that won't catch and break. Heavy-grade corduroys and velvets will show shading, which is not really a sign of wear. Crushed velvet, with its already crushed-in pattern, masks this shading. Vinyls are among

Still another version of modern furniture design exposes the polished chrome frames of the upholstered pieces, covers the matching tables with clear plate glass. Free-form pattern of the rug might be the shadow play of the tossing branches outside; lamp, other accessories lend an Oriental touch.

On these two pages, two versions
of a dream-come-true bedroom.
At left, the magic ingredient
is color, echoed
from the print of the quilt;
the bed is a refinished find;
the table came unpainted.
Opposite, a filmy canopy
over an old-fashionel brass bed
creates an enchanting bower;
fabric also renews the old table.

the longest-wearing materials; better grades are heavy and backed with fabric, usually cotton-knit, to give tear resistance. Silks and satins are beautiful but fragile.

Most fabrics, especially those made from solution-dyed fibers (check the label) are colorfast. But any color can fade if exposed daily to strong sunlight; mixed shades such as blue-green or red-orange may show noticeable color change. Intense colors (turquoise, orange) also tend to fade more and faster.

To guard against water-based and oily stains, many fabrics are treated with a stain-resistant finish such as Scotchgard or Zepel. If the fabric you choose isn't, you can often arrange with the store to have it treated, or do it yourself with spray-on finishes made for home use. But remember that the effectiveness of any finish will gradually diminish with wear, cleaning, and general use. Solid colors and delicate fabrics that are quick to show stain or soil should not be used on furniture subjected to rugged use.

Think about slipcovers

Slipcovers prolong the life of upholstered furniture as well as give it a new look. If you intend to use them at some time, choose your furniture with that in mind. Sofas and chairs with exposed frames and tufted or channel backs are difficult to slipcover, whereas completely upholstered pieces with separate seat and back cushions can be fitted with slipcovers that look as neat as the original upholstery.

When you buy or make slipcovers, be certain the fabric has been preshrunk if you want to be able to launder them. A preshrunk, durable-press fabric that requires little or no ironing is an especially good idea. In considering a patterned fabric, note the size of the pattern unit, or "repeat." If the repeat is large, some fabric waste may be involved in centering it properly on the back and seat cushions. Too large a repeat can also make a small-scaled piece look clumsy. An allover pattern, on the other hand, or a solid color that matches the walls, can disguise an upholstered piece's bad points.

Wood furniture establishes style

Wood furniture, or "case goods," as it is called in the trade, includes tables, side chairs, desks, head and footboards, buffets, cabinets, everything that is not upholstered. Because all its design elements are on view—the shape of a leg, the curve of a chair back, the type of wood and hardware used—it is the more quickly identifiable in terms of style.

For the same reason, its quality is easier to judge. But first let's dispose of the widely believed myth that solid wood is superior to wood veneers. Some of the finest antiques have veneered surfaces. It *is* true that early in the history of mass-produced furniture, veneers

were often ineptly applied, with the result that they eventually warped, cracked, and were known to drop off entirely. Today, improved techniques and better materials (notably, new adhesives) have put an end to all that. Modern veneers can actually add structural strength, as well as beautiful graining, to a piece of furniture. The sketch at the bottom of the page shows how a veneer "sandwich" is put together.

How to judge quality

In the best furniture, you'll find both the finest solid woods and the finest veneers. In less expensive pieces, the woods are less choice but are finished for fine wood effects. To keep costs down, wood substitutes such as particle board (made from wood particles or flakes) are used for out-of-sight elements or in areas such as the sides of a chest where neither stress nor wear is a problem. And more and more furniture manufacturers are using molded plastic elements to replace wood carvings and molding requiring expensive hand labor. When the piece is finished, the plastic is virtually indistinguishable from wood. Also, on tables and chests, plastic-laminate tops provide the look of wood but are much less vulnerable to stains and scratches. (By law, plastic components of wood furniture must be identified on hangtags.)

In top-quality furniture made from fine woods, meticulous hand-finishing techniques are used to bring out the natural grain and color, creating a three-dimensional quality of depth and softness. Less expensive furniture is finished to produce pleasing tones (natural to the wood used or not), and to mask undesirable grain effects, if any. Finishes that have been "distressed" to produce a mellow antique effect can be a practical choice because the distress marks (scratches, "worm" holes, dents) will disguise signs of normal wear.

Here's how to check the construction of a chest of drawers:
• Look carefully at the fitting of all component parts and veneers. Joints should be hairline-thin, nearly invisible.
• Rap the top and end panels with your knuckles; thin panels will sound hollow. Heavy side panels add to the durability of the piece.
• Examine the back. On the best furniture the back panel is recessed to serve as a supporting member. Plywood back panels are stronger than particle board.
• Study the fit of the drawers. Spacing around a drawer should be equal on either side and across the top.

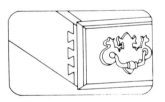

Tightly fitted, dovetailed joints are a sign of a well-made drawer. Further indications: no visible residue of glue; waxing inside and out.

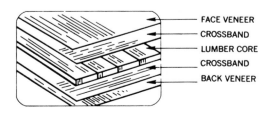

Today's veneers are engineered for extra strength. Cross-banding of grain provides stability, limits expansion and contraction of the particle board core.

FACE VENEER
CROSSBAND
LUMBER CORE
CROSSBAND
BACK VENEER

Here, four brassbound chests, reminiscent of the ones Victorian army officers carried on campaigns, are stacked to create ample bedroom storage space. Each of the units can be used individually in other rooms, perhaps as a coffee or lamp table or a dining-room buffet. Vinyl-coated cork tile on floor reduces noise.

• Pull the drawer out and look for built-in guiding devices that make for easier sliding. Examine the joints of the drawer itself, particularly where front and back meet. You will probably find dovetail joints (see sketch on opposite page); these should be precisely made, fit tightly, and be free of any traces of glue. Run your hand over the interior of the drawer; it should be smooth and completely snag-free. The best drawers are waxed inside and out for easier sliding and for snag-free interiors.

• If the chest has doors, make sure they fit squarely. (But remember that an uneven floor can cause them to hang unevenly. Before rejecting a piece as faulty, make sure it is on an even surface.)

Increasingly today, metals, plastics, and glass are also being used to create functional and strikingly handsome furniture.

planning

CAN SAVE YOU

TIME, MONEY, AND MISTAKES

Furniture should be arranged for convenience, for balance, and for an unimpeded flow of traffic into, through, and out of the room. There are two ways of achieving this. You can move everything about until you are exhausted, or you can measure the room and the furniture and plan your arrangement on paper first. The latter method is a great saver of time and temper. Resorted to before you even buy your furniture, it can produce the best results of all.

How to make a floor plan

If you are moving into a new house or apartment, ask for the builder's plans—but check them for accuracy; changes may have been made after they were drawn up. If no plans are available, make your own. It's easy to do with ¼-inch graph paper, in which each square equals one foot. (A sample sheet is provided on page 247.) You will also need a 6-foot folding wooden rule—the kind carpenters use—to measure with, and a 12-inch straight-edge ruler for marking the dimensions off on your graph paper.

If you already have an accurate floor plan for a room, simply transfer its measurements to your graph paper. If you don't, measure the room from one corner to the next, entering each dimension as you proceed. Then go back and measure windows, arched openings, fireplaces, radiators, built-ins, closets, and doorways. Mark these too on your plan, in their exact locations. All this will give you a clear picture of the available wall space in the room, as well as the traffic lanes for entering and leaving. Indicate these lanes with penciled

Small though it is, this living room accommodates
dining furniture, which also serves to balance
the sofa and chairs. The glass top on the coffee table
creates an illusion of greater space between areas;
floor-to-ceiling draperies, chandelier, add height.
Finishing touch: the red shock of accessories.

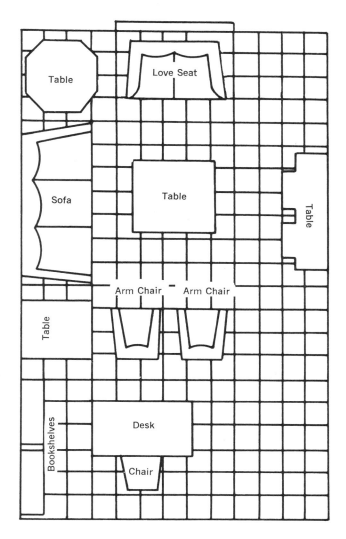

The plan above shows how the gracious, functional
arrangement of furniture in the 13′ x 21′ living room
at left was worked out. Each square on the plan
represents one foot; cutouts of furniture
are in same scale (see pages 245, 249). Longest
unbroken wall is used for sofa; love seat and chairs
complete the conversation grouping.
One large coffee table serves all four pieces;
small benches stored beneath table on opposite wall
provide extra seating. Traffic flows through room
without having to detour around the furniture,
and adequate space is left for entering and leaving.
Note how balance is attained through the use
of unmatched pieces (end tables, love seat, and chairs)
and asymmetrical picture groupings. End of room
(shown on floor plan only) set apart for study
can also serve as an informal dining area.
Austrian shade over sheer curtains controls daylight.

arrows; also show the position of electrical and telephone outlets.

Next measure the width and length of your furniture (or the diameter, if the piece is round), jotting down the dimensions as you work. Then turn to the patterns on pages 245 and 249 and select those nearest to your furniture in size and shape. (If they differ greatly from your pieces, it's best to make your own patterns on graph paper.) Cut the patterns out, or trace them onto cardboard and cut the tracings out.

Now you're ready to plan the room, moving the cutouts around until you know how much furniture will fit comfortably in the available space. First try out the major pieces—the sofa and chairs in a living room, bed and chests in a bedroom. If the room has a natural focal point—a fireplace or a window with a striking view—arrange your major furniture to emphasize it. Next add lamp tables, coffee tables, cabinets, and smaller pieces. Keep the proportions of room and furniture in mind as you work. A tall, narrow piece of furniture usually looks best against a narrow expanse of wall, a long, low piece against a longer one.

Don't forget to allow for unobstructed traffic lanes, at least three feet wide, within the room, and for easy entrance to and exit from it. But unless the room is very small, it's not necessary to line all the furniture up along the walls. Particularly if the room is long and narrow, break it up with furniture that juts out into the room. In a living room of any shape, try to create one or more conversation "islands," with the traffic flowing around rather than through them, and avoid scattering chairs and other seating so far apart that a normal conversational group will find it hard to talk together comfortably. On the other hand, do arrange the furniture to isolate special-interest areas, such as a dining corner or a nook for reading or writing.

Your furniture arrangement should also be well-balanced. That doesn't mean that you have to have matched pairs of everything—chairs, tables, lamps—but only that your furniture groupings, in each

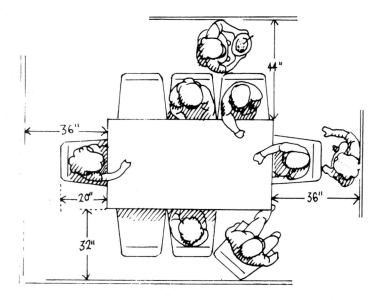

In planning a dining room or dining area, keep in mind the space needed to seat and serve people comfortably. The sketch at left shows minimum requirements for moving a chair out from the table, carrying a serving dish behind a diner, and barely squeezing past. Make sure too that diners have enough elbow room (24 inches is minimum). A round table (opposite) offers an easy solution to this problem. When the table is in use, it is pulled out from window—which, incidentally, boasts a triple treatment, including a shade made from a printed fabric laminated onto regulation shade cloth.

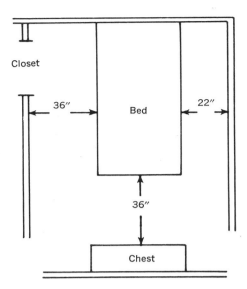

Closet

36"   Bed   22"

36"

Chest

The sketch above shows the minimum space needed
to move about easily in a bedroom. Making the bed
requires at least 22 inches between wall and bed;
opening a chest of drawers or a closet door,
36 inches minimum clearance. Bedroom planning
hinges on your choice of bedding sizes: twin, double,
queen, or king. Queen size is most popular for comfort
and economy; smaller than king but larger than double,
it requires only one mattress-and-springs set,
one bedding wardrobe; twins require two of everything.
When the room is very small, space savers to consider
are a corner arrangement of twin beds
placed at right angles to each other (see pages 228–229),
or, especially in children's rooms, bunk beds
or a single bed with a trundle stored beneath.
A sofa bed, which enables one room to play two roles,
is another good space-saving trick.

This room illustrates maximum use of minimum space.
A sea captain's chest both serves as a lamp table,
provides storage; the dropleaf on the desk folds up
to leave room for passage. Draperies, their pattern
color-coordinated with the rug's graceful design,
extend to almost the full width of the wall.

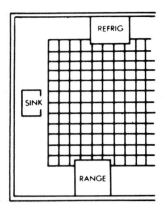

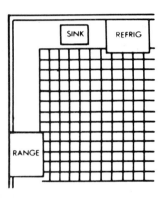

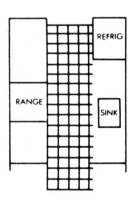

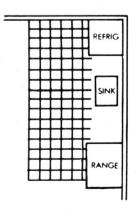

part of the room and in the room as a whole, should seem harmonious. Don't, for example, group all your major pieces on one side unless they are balanced, on another, by an important architectural element, such as a ceiling-to-floor bookcase or a window wall. Study the pictures throughout this book for many different ways to achieve balance in furniture arrangement.

The dimension of height won't show on your plan, but it's important to include it in your calculations. A roomful of furniture at approximately the same level has a monotonous look. Break up the horizontal effect with taller pieces—an étagère, a breakfront, stacked bookshelves. Additional relief can be achieved with floor-to-ceiling window treatments, wall panels, a folding screen, or an overmantel decoration that adds height to a fireplace.

Consider too the relationship between sofas and chairs and the tables that serve them. An end table should usually be level with the arm of a chair or sofa, so a seated person needn't reach up or down to pick up an object. The height of a coffee table is more a matter of preference. (There are some whose height is adjustable.) It goes without saying that any table should be in scale with what it is used with. A tiny table would look absurd beside a massive chair, or holding an oversized lamp.

If your house has an open plan, or if (as is almost always the case), an adjoining room is visible from another, take care to plan the whole area together so there will be a harmonious flow of design as far as the eye can see.

Kitchen planning presents special problems. You'll be confronted with the major ones only if you are building a new house or remodeling an old one, in which case it's advisable to take advantage of the professional kitchen planning services offered by many contractors and appliance dealers. The sketches at left illustrate basic kitchen plans, but many attractive variations (including "peninsula" and

Sketches above and at left illustrate four basic kitchen plans. 1. *U-shaped*. The sink is strategically placed between the range and the refrigerator; continuous counter space links all three. Refrigerator door opens to right. 2. *L-shaped*. The sink and refrigerator are on one side of L, range on the other. Refrigerator door opens to right; corner opposite apex of L is available for dining nook. 3. *Pullman*. Appliances line two sides of a kitchen too narrow to be worked in comfortably by more than one person at a time. Refrigerator door opens to left. 4. *In-line*. All appliances and work space on one side. Used where space is very limited. Many variations of these basic plans are possible. Picture (opposite) shows one: U-shaped with adjoining dining nook.

"island" plans) are possible, depending upon the space available and the amount of money you have to spend.

Today, as in the very first days of this country, the kitchen tends to be the heart of the home. Even an existing kitchen, unless it's very small, can be made to serve more than one purpose by the judicious choice and arrangement of furniture, some of it built-in. A desk tucked into one corner, a portable fireplace in another, a table and chairs or a snack bar with stools can turn a purely functional area into a friendly, inviting room where the cook herself lingers after her work is done.

Incidentally, when you're furnishing your kitchen, it's not necessary to confine yourself to kitchen furniture. The kitchen on the preceding page, and the one on pages 60 and 61, show the attractive effects possible with unconventional pieces—an expedient made eminently practical by today's stainproof finishes and fabrics.

One last word of advice: Play the floor-plan game whenever you want to give a room a new look, not just when you're considering major changes. Often it will show you how the addition (or sometimes the elimination) of a few pieces or the rearrangement of existing ones can improve the room's balance, flexibility, and drama.

On these two pages, two distinctive ways
of using essentially the same basic pieces
produce sharply different effects.
In the small contemporary living room, above,
black-painted étagères placed on each side of the sofa
provide the dimension of height
while forming a harmonious grouping with the paintn'g
they frame. In the larger living room opposite,
similar pieces are placed side by side along one wall;
there, their height, weight, and color
balance the massive painting above the sofa.
Tawny wood-paneled walls, red and gold accents,
create a warmly inviting look. Room above, dominated
by black and white, is cooler, crisper.

A semiformal living room with a versatile furniture arrangement.
The two small coffee tables, used instead of a single large one,
can be moved about as needed; the blue-upholstered desk chair drawn up
to become part of the conversational grouping. Early English style
is here combined with contemporary colors, upholstered comfort.

Good planning makes it possible to utilize every inch of space.
In an apartment living room, free-standing storage units
are stacked to form a dining nook which also doubles as a study.
Shelves hold books, stereo, typewriter; a wall-hung lamp frees table.

Above: A U-shaped arrangement
of three upholstered pieces provides
comfortable seating for six in minimum space.
Built-in bookcases frame the window, create a ledge
for display of decorative objects; free-standing bookcase
backing loveseat in foreground acts as a room divider.
Flooring appears to be wood parquet but is really vinyl.

Left: Large-scale furniture in a small-scale room
looks fine—*if* the arrangement is kept simple. Here,
a wall-hung shelf provides ample display space
for accessories, yet doesn't cramp the style
of massive low-slung chairs and a full-length sofa
(which will later fit equally well into a bigger room).
Neutral backgrounds aid spacious, uncluttered effect.

lighting

MAKES YOUR DECORATING SCHEME
COME ALIVE

Never underestimate the importance of light in your decorative scheme. Light makes colors come alive; color, in turn, affects the quantity and quality of light. White and pale hues reflect most of the light that reaches them, making a room look brighter. Deep hues absorb light, increasing the amount of illumination needed. You have probably noticed too how light borrows color from a surface that reflects it. In a room with a green rug and green draperies, the light itself seems to have a verdant cast to it, like light under the trees in summer.

Because artificial lighting can be planned and controlled, most rooms are more attractive by night than by day. Thinking of lighting in this way, as a decorating tool as well as a practical necessity, will help you make the most effective use of it.

Light sources

There are two basic sources of artificial light—portable lamps and fixtures that are permanently attached to the ceiling or wall. As lighting has become more sophisticated, a third type has been developed that incorporates the light source into architectural elements of the room—a cornice or a ceiling or wall panel. Finally, there is accent lighting, used to highlight a painting (as in the picture on the opposite page), a piece of sculpture, plants, an accessory collection, or any other especially noteworthy feature of the room.

Permanent fixtures and architectural lighting supply what is known as background or general lighting—diffused, indirect light

In this serene traditional room, lighting
plays a dramatic role. The opaque shades
of the Bristol blue oil lamps (here converted
to electricity) cast pools of light on either side
of the fireplace; a tiny spotlight focuses attention
on the painting and the beautifully carved mantel.

COLUMN LAMP. Classic motif appropriate for 18th-century English, Regency, Directoire, and Contemporary furnishings.

Weatherproof spotlights can be installed almost anywhere in a garden to prolong a lovely view after dark.

that reaches the eye after having been reflected off the walls, ceiling, or other surfaces. The direct light needed for reading, sewing, and other close work is usually provided by lamps. Most rooms need both types of light, to serve various needs and to assure a proper balance of light throughout the room. Uneven lighting that results in sharp contrasts and dark corners makes a room seem smaller.

A convenient addition to any room's lighting plan is a dimmer system. With dimmers, you can vary the intensity of the lighting, and therefore the mood of the room, at will. A high level of light is energizing and will motivate guests to go home at a decent hour. If you *want* them to stay longer, try gradually lowering the light to a peaceful, relaxed level.

How to choose background lighting

Architectural lighting is best installed at the time a house is built. There are some types, however, that can be added to existing housing without difficulty. The most popular are in the form of strips of fluorescent tubing, which can be disguised by a cornice, incorporated in a shelf, concealed beneath a countertop, or even combined to create a whole ceiling of light, its brightness controlled by masking the tubing with light-diffusing panels of fiber glass. For dramatic accent lighting, a power track may be mounted to the ceiling or wall (if painted the same color, it will tend to disappear) and individual spotlights clipped on it at any point desired.

Other permanent fixtures are available too, of course—chandeliers, wall sconces, pull-down lights that can be adjusted to any level. Substituted for the often undistinguished fixtures that come with a house or apartment, they can contribute substantially to the usefulness and beauty of a room.

How to choose lamps

The greatest variety of lighting is available in portable lamps. In traditional types the bases are modeled on vases, columns, candelabra, jars, urns, cylinders, and other familiar shapes, as shown in the sketches on pages 130 through 141. You can also have actual vases or other favorite objects wired for use as lamp bases.

For formal traditional rooms, choose classic shapes in porcelain, crystal, bronze, marble, silver, or gold finishes. For less formal rooms,

Architectural lighting is used to fill a contemporary living room with a soft diffused glow. A cornice conceals fluorescent tubes that wash the whole window area with light; a luminous strip extends along the riser for the step up to the piano-study platform, continues under sofa.

Reading in bed is more enjoyable when you have the proper light. Here, a bedside lamp is supplemented by a pair of versatile wall fixtures which can be adjusted to focus light directly on page.

VASE LAMP. This one reproduces a Chinese vase. Others are of classical origin.

bases of ceramic, tole, pewter, brass, wood, or iron are often appropriate, or, in contemporary settings, columns of translucent plastic or free-form shapes in chrome. Shades for formal lamps are usually made of silk or parchment in white or solid colors. Informal shades, of these or other materials, may be white, solid color, or patterned. If you choose patterned or colored shades, you should, of course, consider whether they are compatible with other colors and patterns in the room.

Remember to protect the eyes

There's much more to selecting a lamp than deciding on the decorative effect you want. Since lamps provide the illumination needed for activities that might otherwise strain the eyes, it's important to keep in mind the rules worked out by lighting experts. In general, these amount to a recommendation that, if you use a lamp on a table beside you or on a desk, the bottom of the shade should be slightly above your eye level when you are seated. This is also true for floor lamps.

If the height of the lamp is such that the shape *does* extend below the recommended level, it will help to use a translucent shade that allows a great deal of light to come through, or one that is funnel-shaped to permit the light to spread widely below it. The height of many lamps, both floor and table, is adjustable; look for this feature when buying.

In every case, a lamp shade should be deep enough to shield the eyes of anyone in the room from the bulb, whether he is sitting or standing. (Some lamps have translucent glass bowls that help shade the bulb and diffuse its light.) The width of the shade should be in proportion to the size and shape of the lamp base, but in no case should it exceed the width of the table beneath. If it does, something is wrong—either the lamp is too big or the table too small.

Consider too the different effect of translucent and opaque shades. Translucent shades let some of the light through, adding to the general lighting of the room and appearing themselves as bright areas. Opaque shades concentrate all the light (except that which escapes upward through the opening at the top) on the area below, and are helpful in toning down the brightness of a room with a high level of reflected light. If opaque shades are used in a room where reflected light is scarce, it may be necessary to add more lamps to keep the room from looking gloomy.

Consider the special needs of each room

Since each room of a house is used for a different purpose, each requires a different lighting pattern. If your living room is much used by family and friends for conversation, reading, and games, the lighting should be well diffused and at a rather high level of intensity.

A handsome crystal chandelier
adds sparkle and drama
to a small dining room;
crystal candlesticks contribute
to the elegant mood.
Incandescent bulbs in the chandelier
are controlled by a rheostat dimmer,
making possible any degree
of illumination, from brilliant
to dim. Opaque shades on the bulbs
hide glare from eye and direct light
downwards to the table.

Usually a minimum of five lamps, or an equivalent combination of lamps and fixtures will be required. If the room is also used for television viewing, a dimmer system is ideal for lowering the light to the recommended level. Alternatively, you can use lamps with three-way bulbs and switches.

If your family prefers to do its reading and studying in other rooms, the lighting in the living room can be lower in intensity and opaque shades may be used to accentuate shadow patterns on walls and ceilings and add drama by creating concentrated pools of light.

Dining rooms or dining areas should be lighted according to the

Conventional lighting in this living room above is enlivened by the flickering glow of vigil lights in ruby-colored goblets (visible at far left).

mood of the meal and the diners. A fixture hung from the ceiling, low over the table, creates a dramatic effect. Again, a dimmer is a convenience, making it possible to adjust the light to the situation—low and combined with candlelight for more formal dinners, averagely bright for family meals. One word of caution: Never lower the light to the point that the diners can't see what they are eating; men especially object to this strenuously. Supplement the central light, if necessary, with wall fixtures or cornice lighting. Bulbs in candelabra-shaped fixtures have a more pleasing effect when shades are used with them to direct the light downward.

Bedroom lighting should be planned to suit individual needs. If the

TEXT CONTINUED ON PAGE 140

FIGURE LAMP. Sculpture ranging from classic busts to figures of French court are used for bases. Subject determines the period.

Adjustable shelves turn one wall of a room into a little study. Fluorescent strip lighting concealed beneath the bottom shelf floods the entire desk area; another strip hidden behind cornice at top illuminates book titles.

A luminous ceiling is a particularly good choice
for a bathroom, since it virtually eliminates shadows.
In the bathroom at left, a false ceiling above lavatory
contains fluorescent strips concealed
by frosted white fiberglass in a decorative wood frame.
In the bathroom below, the entire ceiling is luminous,
eliminating the need for any other type of lighting.
"Warm white" tubes used are flattering to skin tones.
Fluorescent strip lighting is mounted
above diffusing panels. In the sketch at bottom,
three incandescent strips are mounted around mirror.

Daylight can also be dramatic

Left: In a garden room, an acrylic skylight floods plants with sunlight they need to thrive, diffuses glare. At night, "eyeball" spotlights, imbedded in each corner of the ceiling, are focused on the growing plants, creating shadowy drama.

Right: Light from a clerestory window fills this room, used as a family room during the daytime, a bedroom at night. Umbrella-shaped ceiling fixture illuminates the reading-in-bed area of both twin beds.

CYLINDER LAMP. Simplest of all lamp shades, it lends itself to varied materials, patterns, and textures.

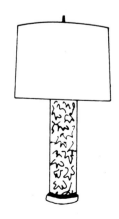

A colorful glass globe,
which can be pulled down
to just the right height for reading,
lights area above a favorite chair
as well as a wall-hung magazine shelf.

occupant often reads in bed, adequate light should be provided by a bedside lamp or wall-hung fixture. Look for lamps with the switch on the base or on the cord, rather than on the upper portion of the lamp where it will be hard to reach. Dresser or dressing-table lights should have white translucent shades and warm white bulbs to illuminate the face evenly and prevent the distortion of skin tones.

Lighting in rooms for small children should be planned for safety. Place lamps well out of the child's reach to avoid the risk of their being knocked over or of the child's touching a hot bulb. Wall fixtures should be firmly attached, and also planned to be out of the child's reach.

Study and work areas have special needs

In areas used for sewing, concentrated study, or extended reading, strong lighting is needed. A pair of lamps (preferably equipped with diffusing bowls) or well-placed wall-mounted fixtures is the absolute minimum.

Another way to light these areas is to mount fluorescent strips on the wall or under a shelf (see picture on page 135). Strip lighting is excellent for sewing if your machine is in a fixed location. If you have a portable, place it in the best position for general overall lighting and focus the light of a floor or table lamp on it.

More general work areas, such as a kitchen, laundry, shop, or hobby room (as well as bathrooms) require ample overall lighting, without shadows, for convenience and safety. Ideally, a kitchen should have several ceiling lights or a completely luminous ceiling, supplemented by additional lighting in food-preparation areas. Here again strip units are extremely useful; installed beneath wall-hung cupboards, they flood the work areas below with light. The same principle of good general lighting, plus concentrated illumination in special areas, should be applied to any room used primarily for work, whatever its nature.

Incandescent versus fluorescent light

For work areas where a high level of illumination is required, fluorescent lighting is recommended, not only because it creates less surface heat but because it is cheaper to operate. For other areas the choice is a matter of personal preference. Incandescent bulbs cast a warm light and, generally speaking, have less of a distorting effect on colors. Fluorescent tubes range from warm to cool in a variety of forms. What is called "warm white" is generally the most effective for home use. "Cool white" or "daylight" tubes are unflattering to skin tones (and to food) and tend to grey or deaden most colors.

In an informal living room, a pair
of figurine lamps are used at each side
of a pleasantly rustic desk,
their opaque shades concentrating
the light on the work area within
the well of the desk. Sufficient
for casual letter writing
or checking household accounts,
the light would need strengthening
for more intense or prolonged work.

JAR LAMP. Most styles
have a charming informality
good for early American
and Provincial settings.
Others may be Oriental.

CANDLESTICK LAMP. Derived from
one of the oldest lighting devices,
it reflects spirit of Colonial decor.

window treatments—

MAKE THEM FOCAL POINTS
OF THE ROOM'S DECOR

Windows have probably been around as long as houses; at any rate we know the ancient Egyptians had them because windows are shown in their wall paintings. The Romans, in the first century A.D., were apparently the first to "glaze," or close these openings with glass. But for centuries thereafter glass was so expensive and so difficult to handle that glazed windows were the exception rather than the rule and were largely confined to the mullioned type—small glass panes held together by lead or wooden strips.

Only in the seventeenth century did glass become cheap enough, and capable of being handled in large enough panes, to make possible the great choice of window types we know today—double-hung, bay, bow, casement, dormer, clerestory, ranch, picture, and window wall, to mention only the most familiar. Along with these many shapes has come a similar variety of ways to treat them.

How to choose a window treatment

The basic purpose of a window, of course, is to let in the light and air, and nothing should be allowed to interfere with that. A good window treatment improves on a window's practical functions, while greatly enhancing its decorative value. The right choice or combination of draperies, curtains, shades, or blinds can control the light, cut down the noise from outside, keep the room cooler in summer and warmer in winter, play up a beautiful view or hide an ugly one. At the same time it provides still another chance to use the magic properties of color,

Room with a view is given a window treatment that controls the light, still lets the outside in. Laminated shades with an Arabian Nights feeling are vinyl-coated, can be wiped clean with a sponge. Strong vertical lines of window frames are repeated in molding that gives architectural distinction to walls.

142

pattern, texture, and proportion in creating an effective decorating scheme.

In choosing a window treatment, consider the following:

• If you want to make the most of a beautiful view, and if too much light is no problem, it's a good idea to leave the glass area uncovered in the daytime. Remember, though, to make provision for covering it at night. Otherwise, unless you have outdoor lighting—or a brilliantly lit big-city backdrop—the window will become a black mirror, cold and uninviting.

• Perhaps you have the opposite problem—an expanse of glass that looks out on a blank wall or into your neighbor's living room. A treatment that lets the light in but cuts the view out, substituting its own decorative interest, is the best solution.

• Does the room get so much sunlight during certain hours of the day that the light must be controlled to prevent glare, excessive heat, or the fading of susceptible fabrics? If so, the window will need shades or blinds of some type instead of or in addition to curtains and/or draperies.

• Do your windows have architectural interest in the form of carved moldings or handsome frames? Then choose a treatment that leaves these elements exposed.

• How about ventilation? Even if your house or apartment is completely air conditioned, you may want to open a window once in a while. Make sure this can be done easily, and that the window treatment does not interfere with the circulation of air.

• Window air conditioners present their own problems. Here again, curtains or draperies should not impede the flow of air. Ideally, too, they may be used to conceal the unit when it is not in use.

• Do you have problem windows—a bow, bay, dormer, or clerestory? Don't despair. There are many ways to handle these and other unusual shapes, as you will see in the following pages. Nor are the solutions all custom-made and expensive. There are readymade treatments and some you can produce yourself.

• Any window treatment should reflect the mood of the room—formal or informal, traditional or modern—and the colors, patterns, and textures used at windows should be carefully coordinated with the rest of the furnishings. Generally speaking, whatever style you choose, the trend today is toward simpler window treatments than in the past.

• Consider how your windows will look from the outside. Though they don't have to be identical, particularly in modern houses, wildly different treatments of nearby windows may produce a helter-skelter exterior look.

An entire glass window wall is curtained
with a light and airy fabric that cuts down glare
without cutting out light. Same treatment can be used
to mask badly placed windows or to create the illusion
that a narrow window extends the width of the wall.

• Before making any decisions, make sure you are aware of the wide variety of styles, colors, and materials currently available. Fabrics for draperies and curtains range from delicate sheers to heavy damasks and brocades; many have a high degree of resistance to light and heat and won't wrinkle easily or at all. Rollup shades come in dozens of different colors and styles, many in hard-wearing, washable vinyl, with decorative trim and pulls. Wooden shutters, shoji panels, Austrian and Roman shades, rollup blinds, new types of Venetian blinds, readymade architectural elements and cornices—these are only some of the possible choices.

How to choose draperies and curtains

Draperies frame the window, covering it completely only when closed. They may be hung from the top of the window or the ceiling line, and reach to the window sill, the apron, or, most formally, to the floor.

Your choice of color and fabric should depend on the decorating effect you want. It pays, however, to consider the possibility of sun-fading. With draperies exposed to strong sunlight, you must expect some, though many modern fabrics are extremely fade-resistant. It may be helpful to keep in mind that sunlight causes a more noticeable color change in mixed shades (blue-green, for instance) than in the primary colors, and in very intense colors, such as shocking pink, than in medium tones. The terms vat-dyed and solution-dyed on labels indicate good colorfastness to light.

Among fibers used for draperies, *fiber glass* is made into many types of drapery fabrics, from very sheer to heavy bouclé and homespun.

Left: Stained wooden shutters are quite in keeping with this Early American room, and are also easy to maintain. These are hinged and louvered for control of light and air; simple curtains and a valance complete the window treatment.

Right: Here, hinged wooden frames, backed by transparent shirred fabric, solve the problem of undistinguished windows and an unattractive view. These continue around a corner, with an opening to adjoining terrace. Fabric, held in place by flat curtain rods, can easily be removed for laundering.

Draperies of fiber glass wash easily, dry quickly, need no ironing, and show virtually no shrinkage. They're also highly resistant to deterioration from strong sunlight. However they do have a few drawbacks—their low abrasion resistance can result in holes and breaks if draperies are allowed to rub against the windowsill or the floor.

Polyester fibers, such as Dacron, Encron, Fortrel, Kodel, and Trevira, are often used for very sheer marquisettes and ninons. These also have easy-care properties and good sun-resistance.

Linen and cotton, often blended with manmade fibers and printed or glazed, are among the most popular drapery fabrics. They usually call for dry cleaning but may be washable if they are unlined. How much they resist sunlight depends a great deal on the fabric type. Fabrics that are loosely woven or made with very fine yarns will be least resistant.

Silk is highly vulnerable to sunlight. Draperies made of silk should always be lined.

Solutions for common window problems

A double-hung window, too small in scale for the wall, is made to seem larger with curtains that extend beyond the frame. With floor-to-ceiling treatment it's even more impressive.

Soften the outlines of a picture window with draw draperies. Or, where less glare, more privacy, are desired, use shades and sheer curtains in wood frames.

Two ways to dress a small window and little-used door: Treat them as one with curtains that open, plus a stationary swag drapery. Or make them twins with cornices, draperies, and Venetian blinds.

Draw draperies that allow access to the sliding door in center are best for this window wall. Clerestory windows like the one shown are usually left uncurtained, since curtains would be awkward to draw.

Linings protect the drapery from soot and sunlight, and give it more body so it hangs well. Lining fabrics should be opaque and tightly woven; cotton sateen is often used. Some lining fabrics are treated with a water-repellent finish that reflects light and heat or that completely blocks out light.

When you buy draperies, check to make sure that the hems at bottom and sides are neatly turned with blind stitching. Bottom hems should be at least two inches deep; the heading about four inches, and backed to give body to pleating. For good fullness and draping quality, the full width of the drapery panel should be just about twice the width of the pleated top. Total width of a pair of draperies should be twice that of the window where they are to be used, plus return and overlap. The diagram on page 165 shows you how to measure a window correctly for whatever type of drapery you choose.

Filigree-patterned hardboard (available at lumber yards) is framed and painted to match walls. On one wall, panels act as cornices for a combination of plain and printed draperies; on another, they frame the bed and at the same time conceal several badly placed beams.

Pumpkin-colored shades
and printed cafe curtains
help make this breakfast room
a sunny retreat. A wooden valance,
flush with the window frame,
adds decorative interest
while it hides shade rollers.
Amusing rooster lamp is emphasized
by the painting behind it,
the pottery figures at its base.

Curtains may be used alone or as a backdrop for draperies. Glass or sash curtains are hung close to the window, on stationary rods, and are usually made of sheer fabrics. They may be tailored, with hems, or finished with ruffles. Tailored curtains are always hung straight; ruffled curtains may be criss-crossed or used with tiebacks. To select correct curtain width, follow this guide: Tailored straight curtains should measure, in total width, 2½ to 3 times the width of the window. Criss-cross curtains: each panel should be twice the window width. Ruffled curtains: each panel should be the full width of the curtain rod. Glass curtains may extend to the sill, the apron, or the floor.

Casement curtains are hung on traverse rods so they can be opened and closed; they extend to the sill or the apron or just clear the floor. Fabrics may be sheer but are usually of a heavier weight than glass-curtain fabrics.

Cafe curtains are hung with rings from cafe rods and may cover the whole window or the lower half only. Or they may be hung in

Glass shelves,
held by brackets
attached to the inside
of the window frame,
display a collection
of thriving houseplants.
Since the plants
are the main attraction
in this window treatment,
draperies and wooden pole
from which they hang
are blue to blend in
with the walls.

Two ways of hiding radiators,
air conditioners, badly placed windows,
or an unsightly view.

Far left: Panels of perforated hardboard,
mounted on a ceiling track, slide open
or closed at a touch. Openwork pattern
(many designs are available) lets in air
and light, closes off eyesores.

Left: Molded fiber-glass arches, backed
by curtains hung from a ceiling track,
handily conceal what's behind them. Arches
come in separate units that fit together;
you can buy as few or as many as needed.

two or more overlapping tiers. They may be made in any fabric weight; usually two or more panels are used at a single window. They may extend to the sill, the apron, or the floor.

Though the fabric may be different, the same fibers used for draperies are also used for curtains, with emphasis on those that are washable and need little or no ironing. Draperies (and curtains) are available readymade in a variety of stock sizes, may be made to measurements you supply, or may be custom-measured and made. If you have a knack for sewing, you can make your own draperies without much difficulty. (See *Good Housekeeping New Complete Book of Needlecraft*.) A variety of readymade accessories, including shirring tape, buckram stiffening, pleater tape, scalloped headings, and edging patterns for shaped cornices simplify the job.

When you want to be able to wash your handiwork, look for materials with a shrinkage-resistance label, or plan to preshrink both fabrics and accessories. If your finished draperies shrink more than three percent, they won't fit your windows after the first washing!

To hang curtains and draperies properly, there is a great variety of handsome hardware. Not only is there a correct type for every purpose, from the simplest of rods for cafe curtains to electrically operated, single- or double-track traverse rods custom curved to fit bow windows, but many types of hardware come in several different materials and finishes: natural or painted wood, pewter, brass or iron, plain or carved or ornamented with intricate designs. Don't forget, in

A shallow bay window forms a nook
for an elegant writing desk
and a Louis XVI armchair. Each window
is treated separately with shade
and draperies, both trimmed
with deep red velvet banding.

choosing the style you like, to make sure the hardware is sturdy enough to do the job that is intended.

Cornices, valances, or *swags* are sometimes used at the top of windows to hide the hardware and create a finished appearance. Cornices may be made of wood or metal. Forms for valances are usually cut from lightweight plywood and covered with fabric, or with padding and fabric for a softer look. Or all-fabric valances may be used. Many cornices and valances come readymade.

How to choose shades, blinds, shutters

If you think rollup shades come only in solid green or white, you're in for a surprise the next time you visit a drapery department. Today they're available in stripes, florals, prints; in a spectrum of colors (there are even some that are one color on one side, a different one on the other); with special trimmings and decorative pulls; in sizes and shapes to fit even problem windows; and with installation brackets that will permit you to do amazing things—like pull a shade up from the *bottom* of the window. And if none of the dozens of standard types suit you, you can have laminated shades made from almost any fabric you choose and treated with a vinyl finish to make it easy to keep clean. (Or make them yourself, using iron-on laminating shade cloth.) Rollup shades may be used alone or combined with curtains and/or draperies or shutters for stunning effects.

Roman and Austrian shades pull up on tapes, rather than roll up. In the Roman type, the fabric forms flat pleats when the shade is raised. Austrian shades create a shirred effect. Both are extremely decorative and may be used with or without draperies.

Venetian blinds, an old standby, are taking on new excitement. They come now with very narrow slats as well as wide ones, in wood,

Wood two-by-fours from lumberyard form the framework for this treatment. Printed fabric shades pull down from above, plain ones pull up from floor, on tracks mounted on inside of two-by-fours, stained to match the furniture wood tones. By varying the colors and the placement of the shades, many variations in design can be achieved.

Hinged and louvered shutters, painted a sunny yellow,
cover a whole window wall. Each pair of shutters
can be opened or closed individually, and the louvers
adjusted to direct light and air upward, downward
or straight into the room. Chair cushions intensify
the shutters' color; louvered door repeats their motif.

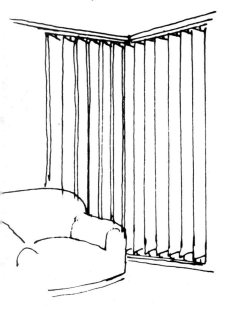

Vertical Venetian blinds, attached to floor and ceiling tracks, are used to unite two awkwardly placed corner windows. As a bonus, they supply the room with architectural interest.

steel, or aluminum, in a range of colors, in different colors front and back, and, on custom orders, laminated with special colors and patterns.

As for shutters, they are made in wood, vinyl, and metal, with solid or movable slats, or with fabric, mesh, caning, or other materials in place of slats. They are perfect for providing privacy and giving a window treatment an architectural look. Handsome enough to be used alone, they can also be used under draperies, over curtains, or above or below cafe curtains.

The pictures and drawings in this chapter illustrate a number of ways to solve special window problems. Here are some further tips:

Solutions for special problems

• Overcome the effect of insignificant or awkwardly placed windows by curtaining the entire wall but arranging the traverse rod to withdraw the curtains from the window area only, leaving the wall covered. The effect produced is that of an entire window wall.

• Mirror panels are marvelous illusion creators. Use them between windows and between the window and the adjoining wall to make a room look bigger and more exciting.

• If you live in an area where outside noise is a problem, double window panes and heavy lined draperies will appreciably reduce it.

• With a floor or perimeter heating system, floor-length draw draperies and curtains may be used. When there is an old-fashioned radiator beneath a window, floor-length draperies should be confined to the left and right of the radiator, and curtains should clear it.

• Clerestory windows over a wall, or a triangular glass gable over a wide expanse of window, are best left uncurtained. To cover them defeats the architectural purpose of windows of this type. There are exceptions to this rule; for example, if you have such a window in a bedroom and are bothered by the early morning light, curtains can be made to cover the area, but it will be difficult to open and close them.

• The success of a window treatment often depends on the careful installation of hardware. If you are installing a rod on dry-wall construction, be sure to find the studs within the wall or ceiling joists for secure anchorage. Sometimes, particularly if the draperies to be carried are very heavy, reinforcing plugs are also needed.

Pierced wooden screens backed by sheer fabric and artificial lighting give room a subtle glow, shut out unattractive view. Effect is enhanced, and size of room seemingly doubled, by mirrored panel behind the gravel-lined tray filled with greenery.

Above: Three-way window treatment
serves several purposes. Cafe curtains
conceal a window air conditioning unit;
Venetian blinds and shade
provide complete light control.
Notice how the bottom edge of the shade
repeats design of the valance edging.

Left: Decorative window molding,
too handsome to cover up, is complemented
by airy tambour-embroidered muslin curtains,
hung on a brass rod within the window frame.
Simple yet elegant, this treatment
is particularly appropriate
with Victorian or French period furniture.

Above: Three narrow windows are united
by a well-planned treatment combining
cafe curtains and window shades. A single
sturdy brass rod holds three pairs of curtains
below individual shades; decorative braid
on the window frames, shades, and curtains
ties the whole scheme together.

Right: A stained glass panel, retrieved
from a dismantled house, is hung
over a fixed center pane in kitchen window.
Decorative panel supplies interest,
does away with need to curtain side casements.
Look for old panels like these
in antique shops, wreckers' yards;
for reproductions, in speciality stores.

Above: An authentic traditional treatment to grace
the most formal of eighteenth-century period rooms.
Under-curtains, hung on a traverse rod,
may be opened and closed. Draperies are trimmed
with fringed braid and tied back with tassels;
the softly draped valance is also fringed and tasseled.

Left: Simpler version of a formal, traditional
window treatment consists of lined draperies,
in a documentary pattern also used for the wallpaper,
tied back over sheer casement curtains. The strips
of the wallpaper and curtains harmonize beautifully
with the color-coordinated floral pattern of the rug.
The furniture has a period French flavor.

Below: Here, matching curtains, fabric, and wallpaper
are used to disguise a high, oddly shaped window.
Curtains are hung cafe style from a brass rod;
when they are closed, the wall line is unbroken.
Windows of this type are often found
in the bedrooms of contemporary houses.

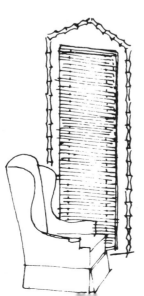

Above: Another way to hide an unattractive view is to use frosted instead of clear glass in windows; it also diffuses light. In this room, Roman shades control the light still further, contribute their subtle pattern.

Far left: Enlarge a window and give it dramatic interest by adding panels at either side. Here, flowered chintz is framed in wood molding for panels; laminated, with protective vinyl coating, onto shade. Matching valance completes scheme.

Left: Window without a frame of its own is given a striking treatment with half-round bamboo molding. (This and other types of molding are available at lumber yards.) Split bamboo blinds, or Venetian blinds with extra-thin slats, add a finishing touch.

Above: Another way to treat
undistinguished windows: front them
with simple wooden frames, covered
with self-adhesive plastic in a marble pattern.
Softly draped valances pick up room colors;
shelf-topped cabinets beneath windows
are covered in the same plastic.

Right: A decorative rattan cornice
adds architectural interest
to a simple window treatment.
Cornices and valances in many colors
and styles come readymade.

Far right: Dormer and other small windows
often look insignificant
when conventionally treated. Here,
decorative braid borders both the wall
around the dormer opening and the Roman shade.

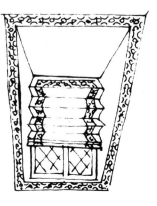

Six ways to treat
a wide or double window

1. Louvered shutters control light and air;
valance at top, cafe curtains at bottom,
add dressing. 2. A single pair of curtains,
hung with brass rings on a brass rod,
is drawn by hand; 3. Cafe curtains
in three tiers, overlapping to conceal
lower rods; 4. Two tiers of unequal length,
one serving as a valance; 5. Two tiers
of equal length, with upper overlapping
the lower. 6. Split bamboo blinds,
paired with cafe curtains at bottom.

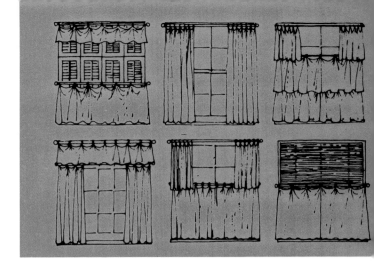

Three ways to
treat French doors

1. Floor-length draperies are hung
from swinging cranes so they don't interfere
with opening of doors. 2. Rods attached
to the top and bottom of each door
hold tightly shirred fabric. 3. Same
treatment as 2, but with curtains
tied in the center with matching fabric.

Three ways to treat
a bay window

1. Draperies on individual traverse rods,
are hung at each window; stationary panels
are used on each side of bay. Valance
on rod attached to ceiling covers top.
2. For a bay with a window seat,
one pair of sill-length curtains is hung
at the center window, another pair
divided between the outer windows.
3. Cafe curtains are used
on all three windows, with floor-to-ceiling
draperies on either side. Bow windows
may be treated similarly, or hung with
draperies on a single curved traverse rod.

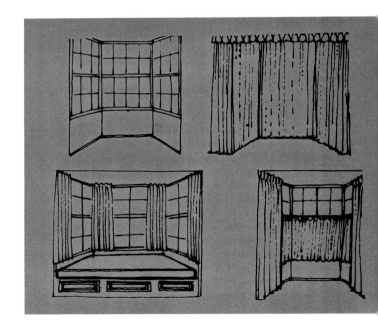

Three ways to treat
a double-hung window

1. For an informal "cottage" effect,
use ruffled curtains and tiebacks.
2. The same window, hung with floor-length
draperies, gracefully draped swag valance,
takes on a formal air. 3. Or an informal
cafe-curtain treatment can be given
width by adding draperies on a rod
that extends beyond the window frame.

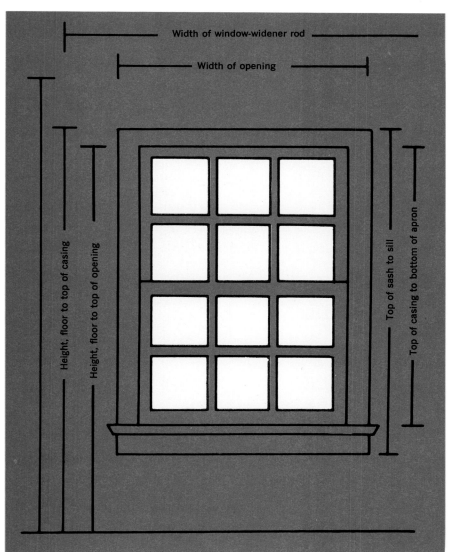

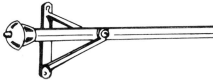

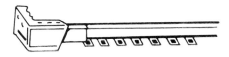

How to measure a window

Use a folding rule or yardstick, and keep your eye level with the point of measurement.

For readymade pinch-pleated draperies meant to meet in the center, the width (measured at the top) should exceed the window width by at least a foot, to allow for a 3- or 4-inch overlap at the point of closure, plus 6 to 8 inches to cover the right-angle turns at the ends of the rod. If you are making your own draperies or curtains, the width of the material should be double or triple the window width (more if very sheer); to the length, add 12 inches to allow for heading and hem.

accessories

GIVE A ROOM CHARM
AND INDIVIDUALITY

The most personal phase of decorating is the choice of accessories. It's the most fun too. Once you've decided on the basic furnishings—carpets, furniture, window treatments—it's time to think about the smaller touches that give a room charm and individuality and reflect your special interests.

How to choose accessories

There are basically two kinds of accessories. Some serve a useful as well as decorative purpose—lamps, for example, clocks, wastebaskets, mirrors, screens, ash trays, pillows, boxes, and dozens of other things necessary to daily living. And then there are things chosen simply because they give pleasure—pictures, sculpture, plants, flowers, and collections of every kind.

Where do you find accessories? Most of us already own things that, with a little imagination, can be used to great effect in accessorizing a room. A pretty little coffee mug can be placed on a desk to hold pencils; wine coolers and ice buckets make handsome containers for flowers or leaves; seldom-used vegetable dishes can be converted to planters; shells picked up at the beach or rocks found on country walks can be arranged to add interest to any room; a handsome saucer or plate may make a much prettier ash tray than a piece specifically designed for the purpose.

When you have exhausted this source, the outside possibilities are endless. Department stores, thrift shops, charity bazaars, curiosity and antique shops, art galleries, museums are only a few places to look.

A collection of Early Americana—wind toys, weathervanes and signs—is skillfully arranged on the wall of a small entrance hall, with a potted palm contributing balance to the grouping. If displayed with imagination, any collection can be used to decorative advantage.

Pictures, a wooden figurehead, candle sconces, a rooster silhouette, are combined to form an interesting arrangement above a credenza. Notice the balancing of shapes careful within the confines of the piece of furniture below, which provides the grouping with a straight bottom edge.

Don't limit yourself just to art museums either; often the gift shops of state or county historical societies, natural history museums, and industrial museums have fascinating treasures to offer, from old weathervanes to exotic minerals. Travel offers a chance to bring back souvenirs—wood carvings, masks, wall hangings, figurines.

When it comes to choosing pictures, ignore the absurd notion that an original oil painting is superior to other forms of art. Besides oil paintings, there are available, usually at lower prices, water colors and drawings, as well as "original" prints—original, that is, in the sense that the artist himself prepares the printing surface—a metal plate, stone slab or wood block—and a limited number of copies are reproduced. Then there are photographic copies of paintings, drawings and

Here one whole wall of a living room is devoted to pictures of all sizes and types—lithographs, oils, collages, watercolors—in an arrangement that keeps the outside edges aligned on all four sides. Benches below are used to display other accessories.

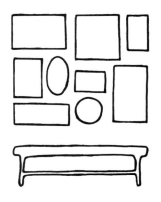

Three different methods of arranging pictures: At right, pictures of various sizes and shapes are hung so their outside edges form a square. Far right, pictures are aligned at sides and top only, with furniture balancing the grouping. Below, in a symmetrical arrangement, the bottom edges are aligned.

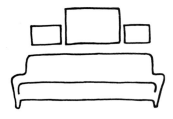

prints. A good original work of art is a joy to have and may increase in value over the years. But there are many bad ones around too; in lieu of these, it would be better to buy good reproductions.

Create your own accessories too, drawing on skills you already possess or can acquire without great difficulty. Try your hand at needlepoint for strikingly beautiful seat covers, wall hangings, pillows, bell pulls. Or use easy-to-follow stamped or transfer appliqué or embroidery patterns to decorate draperies, linens, pillows. Or work with ceramics, decoupage, flower arranging, water colors, oil paints. (For books on these crafts, see page 243.)

Overall, there are no rigid rules to follow in choosing accessories, just a few basic guides. One is to select things that reflect your own tastes and interests. Another is to keep your color scheme in mind. Accessories can supply a needed bright accent, or, in a room full of bright colors, provide a welcome rest for the eye. Don't hesitate to combine old things with new, but do make sure they share the same mood—formal or informal, simple or sophisticated.

How to arrange accessories

Consider first whether the proportions are right. A piece of sculpture or a lamp should not dwarf the table it stands on; a picture shouldn't seem utterly insignificant in comparison to the sofa over which it is hung. (The latter problem can be overcome by grouping several pictures together, as shown above.) The texture and shape of accessories,

Pictures and other accessories that echo the room's color scheme complement wall-hung cabinets in a light-hearted, young-looking dining room. Decorative sconce adds interest; philodendron and daisies contribute live touch.

In an Early American living room, carefully chosen accessories sound a warmly authentic note. Lamp bases are antique ceramic jugs; a duck decoy and a tea canister share the mantel with a primitive portrait. The documentary print used for the draperies carries on theme.

as well as their color, should be taken into account, and satisfying contrasts or harmonies worked out. Collections should be displayed together, for maximum impact. Try grouping them in a lighted cabinet or a shadowbox, on open shelves, in a glass-covered recess in a tabletop, or hang them on pegboard, on a screen, or directly on the wall. Table and desk tops should not be so cluttered with accessories that they can't be used.

The arrangement of pictures is an art in itself, but it is one that can be easily learned. While one large picture may be all that is needed over a sofa (see opposite page), smaller pictures and other objects are best displayed in groups. The photographs on pages 168 and 169 and the sketches on page 170 illustrate several ways of doing this, all based

on the principle of keeping the outside edges aligned. Asymmetrical balance, as shown in the grouping of pictures and a clock, below at left, and of primitive folk art on page 167, is also effective, but somewhat harder to bring off.

A method of picture arranging often used by professional decorators is first to place the pictures on a large piece of brown paper on the floor. Move them around until you like the way they look, then outline the frames on the paper and mark the points where picture hooks will be needed to meet the wire on the backs of the frames. Now tape the paper lightly to the wall where the pictures are to go, and nail the hooks to the wall right through the paper. All that remains is to remove the paper and hang the pictures.

In another room with an Early American feeling, contemporary versions of antique accessories blend well with a semi-abstract painting. Note the asymmetrical arrangement on the wall above the lamp table, with the lamp itself becoming part of the grouping.

A well-planned wall system
adds decorative interest
while serving many purposes.
Shelves display books
and accessories; cupboards
and drawers store glassware
and other dining needs.
Top of unit serves as a wine rack,
lower portion as a buffet.

Various rooms have various special needs. Accessories for a living
room might include, in addition to lamps, pillows, and wall decorations, ash trays (even if you don't smoke your guests may); small
china or silver trays that can double as coasters for beverages; several
boxes (wood, metal, crystal, or china) for storage of cigarettes,
candies, and other small items. To these you might add a piece of
sculpture, a plant or flowers, a clock, a book or two, magazines, or a
collection—glass paperweights, mounted butterflies, antique toys—
that you or a member of your family has assembled.

If the room has a fireplace, like the one at the right, you might well
make its mantel decoration the focal point of the room. This is a good

In a room George Washington would have felt at home in,
a collection of ironstone china is displayed
in a hutch cupboard; brass candlesticks
of various sizes and a Staffordshire statuette
grace the mantel; antique iron lion guards the fireplace.

place for your most important picture or a beautifully framed mirror or a handsome clock flanked by greens or flowers or by candlesticks or electrified candelabra. Look at examples in pictures throughout this book; the Index (under "Mantels") will help you find them.

Hearth tools are also important accessories. Choose simply styled brass or black wrought iron for early American or other provincial rooms; more ornately designed brass and bronze for formal period rooms; iron, brass, chrome, or bronze with contemporary styling for modern settings. Fireplace screens are essential for safety; fenders create a finished look.

The dining room is the place to display your best china, crystal, silver, or pewter. The table is usually left bare between meals except for an arrangement of flowers or fruit or an attractive tureen or covered dish in proper scale with the table. On a sideboard you might use a tray holding a tea or coffee service, candlesticks, or crystal decanters for wine or liqueurs. If you have a breakfront, corner cupboard, hutch or china cabinet, use it for a pretty collection of

Left: This corner cupboard
holds a colorful display of pitchers
of all sizes and shapes, ranging in date
from the eighteenth century to present-day
reproductions of older types. In arranging
a display like this, resist the temptation
to crowd too much in; leave enough space
so each object can be clearly seen.

Right: In this contemporary living room,
a collection of colorful pillows, round,
square and bolster-shaped, are used
to handsome effect on a divan.
Even magazines and newspapers,
rolled and stored in a wicker wine basket,
can serve as decorative accessories.

Above: Accessories that are both beautiful
and practical grace a desk.
The lamp is tall enough to shed light
over the whole working area,
traditionally styled to match the furnishings.
The antique box holds writing equipment,
stamps; flower vase is a copper pitcher.
The cut-leaf philodendron and ornate clock
at right of desk, and the painting above it,
complete the corner grouping.

Right: In this room, several
of the most striking accessories—
the framed face-in-the-sun, two pillows,
the rug, and the footstool's covering—
are all needlepoint, products
of the owner's skill. The tortoiseshell
pattern of the lamp shade
is echoed in the box on the coffee table,
the classic shape of the lamp base
in the pair of columns beside it.

plates, pitchers, cups and saucers, goblets—anything of special interest that is related to dining. A pleasant, simple treatment for a dining room is shown on page 171.

In the bedroom, again start with the essentials—good lamps and lighting fixtures, at least one mirror, perhaps a bedside telephone, a clock or clock radio, a wastebasket, a tray for perfume bottles, covered boxes to hold various small objects that might otherwise clutter dresser or tabletops.

Sheets, blankets, and bedspreads are also considered accessory items and can contribute greatly to the character of the room. The variety in sheets and pillowcases is enormous; they come in a rainbow of colors and in many patterns: polka dot, stripe, plaid, floral, toile. Bedspreads, both custom- and ready-made, colorful regular and electric blankets, and decorative pillows offer further opportunities for turning an ordinary bedroom into an inviting retreat. Family photographs, pictures, personal collections, trinkets of special interest to the occupant are all wonderful bedroom accessories; so are plants or an arrangement of flowers or leaves.

The bath is the one room that depends almost entirely on accessories for glamor and comfort; strangely it is also the room most usually neglected in accessorizing a house. There's no need; the array of coordinated colors and patterns in bath towels, shower curtains, and rugs can make the plainest bathroom look exciting. In addition, try putting an interesting frame around a stock mirror; use "unbathroomy" lighting fixtures—a chandelier, electrified gas lamps, wall sconces; investigate the many different designs in faucet fixtures. There is never enough storage space in a bathroom; install open shelves and brackets to hold attractively packaged toiletries, pretty containers for soaps and other necessities, stacks of colorful towels. Extra towel bars and rings, a hamper, a small bench or stool, a transistor clock, and a bathroom scale are great conveniences, a wall-telephone pure luxury. Plants such as fern, ivy, or philodendron thrive in the moist atmosphere of a bathroom, if they are placed near a window for light.

The kitchen offers more possibilities for fun with accessories than any other room, especially for the cook who likes to have all her tools and equipment out within plain sight and easy reach. The kind of cook who enjoys the variety of colors and textures of cookware—copper, porcelain, iron, stainless steel, glass. The kind who loves the pattern and textures of vegetables in bins, fruit in bowls, growing herbs in pots, glass jars of beans, lentils, pastas, nuts, and other foods. Given half a chance, a kitchen will accessorize itself. To aid in the

Not all pictures are painted with a brush. This one is done in bold strokes of yarn against a background of cotton homespun. Kits, which include yarn, needle and stamped fabric, make it easy to produce big, important pieces like this one. Urn-shaped lamp and other accessories show it off to best advantage.

Most bathrooms would look drab without accessories,
and the one above is no exception. Towels, rug,
and shower curtain spice the beige-toned tiles;
a molded terra-cotta stool adds additional color.
Stag's head fern thrives in the humid atmosphere.

Bathroom accessories can be pretty
as well as practical. Use glass jars
to hold necessities like cotton swabs;
try an attractive saucer as a soap dish.
Wooden dowels make unusual towel holders.

The handsome gold-framed mirror
in this powder room forms door of the medicine
chest; the towel colors are coordinated
with the wallpaper. Crystal light fixture,
dried-leaf arrangement, are added touches.

process, there are handy pegboard panels and special-purpose hooks for hanging almost anything—pots and pans, a cookbook holder, kitchen utensils, towel racks. Canister sets come in a great variety of colors and patterns in copper, ceramic, aluminum, wood, lacquered tin. A spice rack can be as handsome as it is handy, while framed pictures or prints that wipe clean are worth having as a feast for the eyes alone. A kitchen is also the place for food-oriented collections such as unusual rolling pins, copper molds, old wooden cookie presses.

Even if your kitchen is too small for much display, or if you prefer to store supplies and equipment neatly out of sight, don't forget such vital accessories as a clock, wastebaskets, a shelf for cookbooks, a bulletin board, and, if possible, a wall-hung telephone.

Kitchens offer a fascinating opportunity to display handsome and useful accessories. Here, two different approaches: In the contemporary kitchen at left, accessories are chosen for their clean, simple lines—jars in streamlined shapes holding dried foods are lined up on the window ledge; above the cupboards, plants and cookbooks frame a beautiful decanter. In the early American version at right, copper pots, molds, woodenware, and containers in traditional shapes make up the decoration.

In any room in the house, don't forget accessories that add life, color, movement. House plants are wonderful for that, and there are many varieties to choose from—plants for sunny windows, plants for darker rooms, plants that flower, plants with patterned foliage, plants that grow as big as small trees, plants that make graceful vines. Your florist or nurseryman can tell you all about the light and moisture needs of the various kinds and help you choose.

Use fresh flowers for accessories whenever you can; leaves, dried flowers or grasses, or beautifully shaped bare branches also make interesting arrangements. A bird in a cage, an aquarium full of colorful tropical fish, wind bells, mobiles, a clock with an audible tick, a fire in the fireplace—these add life and movement too and can be a constant source of interest.

table settings

PROVIDE A DAILY CHANCE
TO BE CREATIVE

Table settings offer, each day, a fresh chance to add beauty and interest to your home. They can also make every meal an occasion, whether it's a simple breakfast served on place-mats or a formal dinner gleaming with crystal and silver. The important ingredients are imagination and the necessary tools—carefully selected dinnerware, glassware, flatware, and table coverings.

Speaking of imagination, don't confine all your meals to the dining room or dining area. On a winter day, eat breakfast near a sunny window, dinner by a fireplace; on a fine summer day, outdoors. For lunch, arrange attractive trays, to be taken anywhere in the house. Occasionally serve dinner buffet-style in the living room. If you have small children, you may not be able to vary family meals in this way, but do be flexible in your arrangements for guests.

Choosing dinnerware

It's easy to be overwhelmed when you visit the dinnerware department of any store and are faced with the vast selection available. Although, today, all dinnerware is loosely referred to as "china," there is actually considerable difference among the various types.

CHINA (the true kind, also called porcelain) is made of fine clays fired at very high temperatures. The result is a translucent white, non-porous dinnerware that rings like a bell when tapped. It is highly resistant to chipping and cracking; it is also relatively high in price, owing to the care that must be taken in its manufacture. Until the

In a traditional dining room furnished with antiques, fine silver, china, and glassware are displayed against beautiful bare wood. A crystal chandelier, branched candelabra, and candles in hurricane shades throw a softly flattering light over all.

186

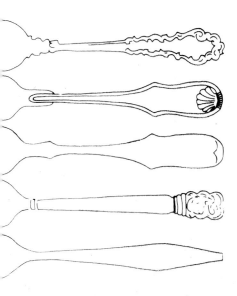

Patterns in silver flatware
range from baroque
to starkly simple in both
traditional and modern
designs. In sketches above,
the top three patterns
are considered traditional;
the bottom two contemporary.

eighteenth century, when European makers learned the secret, all such fine ware was imported from China; hence its name. Today it is made in many countries. Bone china, made by adding bone ash to the clay, is particularly noted for its whiteness and translucency; most of it comes from England.

EARTHENWARE is made of unrefined clays fired at lower temperatures, and is more porous, under the glaze, and less resistant to chipping and cracking than fine china. Often called semiporcelain or semivitreous ware, earthenware varies in thickness; some is almost as thin as china. But it doesn't let light through, as fine china does, or have china's clear bell-like ring. Sometimes called pottery, earthenware is usually lower in price and almost always decorated with colorful informal patterns. Many primitive designs of great charm can be found in this category. Stoneware, or ironstone china, is a heavier ware with excellent wearing qualities, occasionally decorated in color but more often with designs formed by embossing plain surfaces.

MELAMINE is an extremely tough plastic dinnerware. Like other dinnerware, it can withstand the heat of a dishwasher, and it is highly resistant to chipping or cracking. Over a period of time, it *will* show knife scratches. For this reason, a patterned surface is a better choice than a plain one, and a light color better than a dark.

GLASS-CERAMIC TABLEWARE, sometimes called oven-to-table china, can stand extremes of hot and cold and has high breakage resistance.

The type of decoration also affects the wearing qualities of dinnerware. Underglaze decoration is applied, either by hand or by a transfer method, before the piece is dipped or sprayed with a ceramic glaze. Firing fuses the glaze to the clay. The colors and designs are thus protected by a hard, transparent coating, and are less likely to deteriorate from wear, abrasion, or washing than is overglaze decoration, which is added after the glaze has been fired. (Gold, silver, and platinum decorations can only be applied overglaze.) You may, however, wash dinnerware with overglaze decoration in a dishwasher, if you omit the detergent.

What type of dinnerware should you choose? That depends on your preference and your pocketbook. There is a range of prices in each category, depending on the design and the care taken in manufacture. Ideally, it's nice to have one set of dinnerware for fairly formal occasions, another for more casual use. If you are limited to one service,

On the opposite page, at top, contemporary flatware
is used with a French Provincial earthenware design;
simplicity of both makes them good companions. At bottom,
hobnail glasses, Early American in origin,
go equally well with contemporary dinnerware, wood-handled
stainless-steel flatware, and gay flowered placemats.

For variety, try serving meals all around the house. Here, a buffet supper is arranged on a slate-topped coffee table in a contemporary living room. Dinnerware and serving pieces are modern copies of traditional Chinese-export porcelain.

choose a formal pattern; it will be usable on all occasions. And unless you have young children don't hesitate to use fine china every day if you like. However delicate it may seem, it can withstand a great deal of wear.

Fine china is sold by the place setting or in sets; less expensive ware usually comes only in sets. A 5-piece place setting consists of dinner plate, salad plate, bread-and-butter plate, cup, and saucer; a six-piece setting adds a soup plate or cup. Serving pieces might include platters, vegetable dishes, sugar and creamer, butter dish, and sauceboat; these need not be of the same pattern if you prefer to mix rather than match. "Open stock" means that additional pieces may be bought later—but only so long as the store stocks your pattern or the manufacturer continues to make it. Traditional patterns in fine china are more likely to be continued than others. In any service, cups and saucers seem to suffer the most breakage, so it is wise to buy extra sets of these in the beginning.

How to select flatware

Flatware is the general term for knives, forks, spoons, and serving pieces; in this too there is considerable choice.

STERLING SILVER flatware is 85.2 percent pure silver; the rest is copper, added for strength and hardness. Sterling can be used daily for centuries without wearing out; in fact, use adds to its attractiveness by giving it a soft sheen called a "patina," and reduces the need for polishing. Even if a sterling pattern is discontinued, you can often order additional pieces during the manufacturer's slack season.

Sterling is most often sold by the place setting, which usually consists of knife, fork, salad fork, teaspoon and dessert (or soup) spoon. In a six-piece setting, a butter spreader is added.

Another way to dine—this time formally—in a living room. Three tables, cleared of daytime accessories, surround the sides and back of the sofa, creating ample space for six sitdown diners. Silver candlesticks lend elegance.

Imagination is all-important
in creating centerpieces.
Here, white pottery containers
that stack are filled
with common garden flowers.

Serving pieces, which might include tablespoons, carving knife and fork, gravy ladle, sugar spoon (or tongs), and extra pieces, such as fish knives and forks and iced-tea spoons, are sold separately. Sterling prices vary with the design, weight and workmanship.

SILVER PLATE, which is considerably less costly than sterling, is made by applying a coating of silver to a base metal. In the better grades, the coating is thicker, and is reinforced at wear points. Good silver-plated flatware can last for a lifetime. It is usually sold in sets rather than by place setting.

VERMEIL once consisted of sterling silver plated with gold and was consequently very expensive. Today it is made by applying the gold to a base metal and is available at reasonable cost.

STAINLESS STEEL comes in the widest quality range of all, from inexpensive light ware to weighty, beautifully designed pieces with the soft sheen of silver. It is sold either by the place setting or in sets. Like vermeil, stainless steel never needs polishing.

Hollowware, which consists of serving dishes and accessories such as platters, trays, vegetable dishes, candlesticks, salts and peppers, and the like, comes in sterling silver, silver plate, Sheffield silver (silver-coated copper), stainless steel, and pewter. Although, if you have a full dinnerware service, your need for hollowware may be limited, it is a handsome addition to any table. Stainless steel hollowware, unlike the flatware, comes only in modern designs. In other hollowware, both traditional and modern patterns are represented.

How to select glassware

Attractive glassware makes a table sparkle; it is available in every price range. Tumblers or footed tumblers for water, juice, and iced tea are usually used for family meals and informal entertaining; stemware (water goblet, sherbet/champagne glass and all-purpose wine glass) for formal occasions. Cocktails, aperitifs, and liqueurs call for various special glasses. Individual glass finger bowls (usable for salads and desserts), glass dessert plates, and glass accessories such as salts and peppers, a water pitcher, and a salad bowl are also nice to have.

When you're shopping for glassware, you'll be confronted by a maze of terms. Here, to clear up the confusion, are a few basic facts:

"CRYSTAL" has a characteristic brilliance and, when tapped, a clear bell-like tone. Also called "lead crystal," it is actually fine glass to which lead oxide has been added.

In a corner of a contemporary family room,
a pedestal table and bentwood chairs are used
for informal dining as well as for games. The table
is set for lunch; the simple fruit centerpiece
can be admired now, eaten later. Notice how the green
of two chairs, curtains, is picked up in napkins, goblets.

Here, a buffet supper
is served on a passthrough
counter; diners
take their plates
to a table in the family room.
Flowers add festive grace
to this or any meal.

COLORED GLASS is made by adding small amounts of other metal oxides to clear-glass mixtures—copper for green, cobalt for blue, iron for amber. Milk glass is opaque; it comes in pastels as well as white.

HAND-BLOWN GLASS is made by skilled craftsmen who take a blob of molten glass on the end of a blowpipe and form it into the desired shape. Today hand blowing is used mostly for fine stemware and decorative glassware. Most tableware is produced by machine, though embellishments such as gold bands or enameled designs may be added by hand.

PRESSED GLASS is produced by pouring molten glass into a mold. It can be made by hand or machine. Sometimes the mold is elaborately decorated, producing what is known as *patterned* or *Sandwich* glass (from a nineteenth-century glass factory in Sandwich, Massachusetts).

CUT GLASS has a sculptured, textured design, produced, in the best grades, by hand. The goblet or other object is held against small, revolving abrasive wheels; the pattern thus produced has more clarity than pressed-glass designs.

Table coverings and centerpieces

If your tabletop is exceptionally attractive—highly polished wood or sparkling glass—you need not cover it with anything. Or you may use place mats, or stainless steel, pewter, glass, or china service plates. If you do use a tablecloth, it should go over a pad and hang down 12 to 16 inches below the tabletop. Formerly a white damask or lace tablecloth was considered the only acceptable covering for formal entertaining. Now you may use any color that suits your mood and

The color and character of the dinnerware should be considered in selecting table linen. This cloth matches the blue of the pottery; the napkins repeat the marigold color.

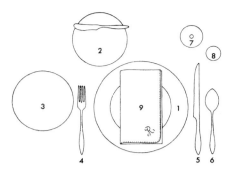

Informal dinner setting

1. Dinner plate
2. Bread-and-butter plate
   with butter spreader
3. 7″ or 8″ plate for salad
4. Dinner fork, to be used
   for both main dish and salad
   (or place a salad fork to right
   or left of dinner fork,
   depending on whether salad
   is to be served before
   or after entree)
5. Dinner knife
6. Dessert spoon
7. Water glass
8. Juice glass
9. Dinner napkin
Place coffee spoon on the saucer
when coffee is served

How to set a table

Flatware should be placed
in order of use, working from
the outside toward the plate.
Turn the cutting edge of knives
toward the plate. Water glass
goes directly above the knife;
other glassware is placed to right
of the water glass. Fold
and place napkins to left
of the fork or on the plate.

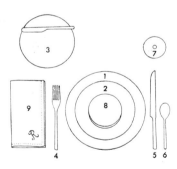

Luncheon setting with first course in place

1. 9″ plate for main course
2. 7″ or 8″ plate
3. Bread-and-butter plate
   with butter spreader
   across top
4. Luncheon fork, to be used
   for both main dish and for salad
5. Luncheon knife
6. Teaspoon for fruit cocktail;
   substitute soup spoon
   if first course is soup
7. Water glass
8. Fruit-cocktail glass
9. Luncheon napkin

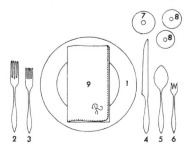

Formal dinner setting

1. Service plate
2. Dinner fork
3. Salad fork
4. Dinner knife
5. Soup spoon
6. Oyster fork for seafood
   cocktail
7. Water goblet
8. Wine glasses
9. Dinner napkin

The spirit of Queen Victoria still reigns
in this dining room, where the table is set
for a family dinner. Blue-and-white wall covering
establishes the color scheme; strongly patterned cloth
sets off the dainty china, porcelain-handled knives.

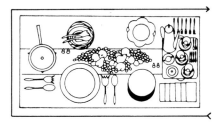
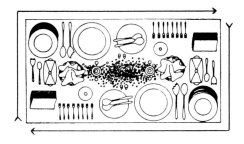

How to set a buffet

In sketch 1, the buffet
is set up against a wall,
with centerpiece out of the way
of service. In sketches 2 and 3
tables are in the center of room,
with traffic moving around them.
Sketch 2 shows a single lane,
sketch 3 a double one, useful
for expediting service
when there are many guests.

coordinates with your tableware; fine linen, lace, or organdy place
mats are also appropriate.

In choosing table coverings, consider the character of your tableware. If it's contemporary, you can use either bright solid colors or a
modern design; if it's traditional, you may prefer white or pale colors
or a traditional pattern. A patterned table covering should harmonize
with the pattern, if any, of the dishes. Cloth napkins should be used
for all but the most casual meals. Dinner napkins should be large, 18
to 24 inches square, especially for buffet or tray meals.

For centerpieces, use fresh flowers in season, a flowering houseplant
in a decorative container, even just a blossom or two floating in a bowl
of water. Fresh fruit also makes an appealing centerpiece: polished
apples in a wooden bowl; an arrangement of peaches, pears and
nectarines; green grapes and a pineapple in a silver epergne. Even
fresh vegetables to be cooked and eaten tomorrow can be today's
centerpiece. Try an all-green arrangement of peppers, cucumber, and
broccoli in a wooden bowl, or mix colors and shapes: squashes, gourds,
cauliflower, eggplant. Appropriate accessories—a handsome covered
tureen, for example—can be used alone as centerpieces.

For easy across-table conversation, keep centerpiece heights below
the eye level of seated diners. Candle flames should be above or below
eye level, never directly in line.

Traditional Meissen-pattern plates
dominate the buffet at right,
establishing a blue-and-white
color scheme. Here, the flatware,
napkins, and plates
are all picked up first;
guests then help themselves
from the silver chafing dish.

Variety is the key to the most effective table decoration. Unmatched extra pieces of china and silverware, unusual glassware, accessories in wood, pottery, pewter—the ways to add character and interest to table settings are as unlimited as your imagination. Look for accent pieces in antique shops and flea markets, at rummage sales and church bazaars, as well as in department and specialty stores. Mix old and new; combine shapes, colors, and textures as you choose. Above all, dare to experiment. The only rule here is the same one that governs other aspects of decorating: unless you are deliberately aiming at the shock of surprise, try to keep the mood the same. A Toby jug filled with wild flowers would be a charming centerpiece for an informal meal; in a formal setting it would be out of place. Similarly, elaborate silver candlesticks might look inappropriate if used in a starkly modern setting.

In a dining room with an Empire feeling, twin marble-topped tables with twin candelabra offer versatile possibilities for dining. Each table can accommodate four people in intimate ease, each can be used alone or in tandem. Range of colors on chair cushions enlivens the black-and-white color scheme.

storage

LETS YOU KEEP THINGS
UNDER CONTROL

Rare is the household, big or small, that has enough storage space. Whether you live in a Victorian mansion or a modern split-level, keep house just for two or have a pride of children, it's highly probable that your possessions outnumber the places to put them. Unless something is done about it, the result can spoil the best decorating plan.

The first step in solving the problem—as many others in life—is to make the most of what you have. Often you can double the capacity of existing closets by *organizing* the space. Double-decker clothes rods, with space on the upper level for blouses, jackets, and shirts, on the lower for skirts, pants, and slacks, is a good closet organizer. So are shoe racks, tie and belt holders, garment bags and boxes, and boudoir chests of drawers.

Second, look for places to install extra closets. (You can buy these prefabricated; they are shipped knocked down, ready to assemble.) Likely sites might be a stairwell, a hallway, or wall space on either side of a window (for extra mileage, fill the embrasure thus created with a chest that serves both for storage and, with a cushion on top, as a window seat). Or assemble a whole storage wall. It need not take much space from a room. What's more, if you fit it with sliding doors of mirror glass, you will immediately seem to double the room's size. Or, in a house with an open plan, you can use a storage wall as a room divider.

Consider too the many uses of wall systems—shelves, chests, and cabinets in various combinations. These come painted or unpainted, in fine furniture finishes, in stainless steel, clear or opaque plastic; they

A storage wall can be designed to accommodate
the needs of any activity. On the opposite page,
space is provided for sewing essentials.
When not in use, the work table folds up;
its support both acts as a bulletin board
and carries out the vari-colored pattern of the wall.

Left: Decorative storage space is gained in a small living room by means of built-in bookcases with cupboards beneath. The two units flank an antique chest (which also serves for storage), creating an attractive niche and adding architectural interest to the room.

Opposite: Here, one section of a family-room wall is designed to suit several purposes. A small sink and refrigerator are useful for serving beverages; both can be hidden behind the folding wooden screen. Likewise, the television set above the sink can be screened by sliding wooden panels. Above the desk is a receiver for AM-FM stereo. Speakers are at ceiling height; one above the desk, the other over the yellow cupboard.

may be free-standing or fastened to the wall; you can order them custom-made or assemble them yourself from stackable units. They are handy for storing everything from books and stereo equipment to china, linen, and bedding.

To restore order to a chaotic basement or seasonal closet, investigate such utilitarian aids as metal shelves and fiberboard wardrobes. A lumber dealer is a good source of materials and sketch plans for simple do-it-yourself storage units of all types. For ingenious readymade solutions, check mail-order catalogues and the unfinished furniture departments of local stores.

Another good storage idea is pegboard, also called perforated hardboard (install it over ½-inch furring strips to allow clearance for hooks). Pegboard comes printed with a wood grain, covered with a fabric-like surface, prepainted, or ready to be painted any color you choose. Use it in a kitchen to store pots and pans, towels, a cookbook shelf; in a mud or utility room for outdoor clothing, boots, shovels, brooms; in a child's room for toys and sports equipment; in a garage for auto accessories and garden tools.

In this chapter you'll find a number of ways to solve specific storage problems. See if they don't give *you* some good ideas!

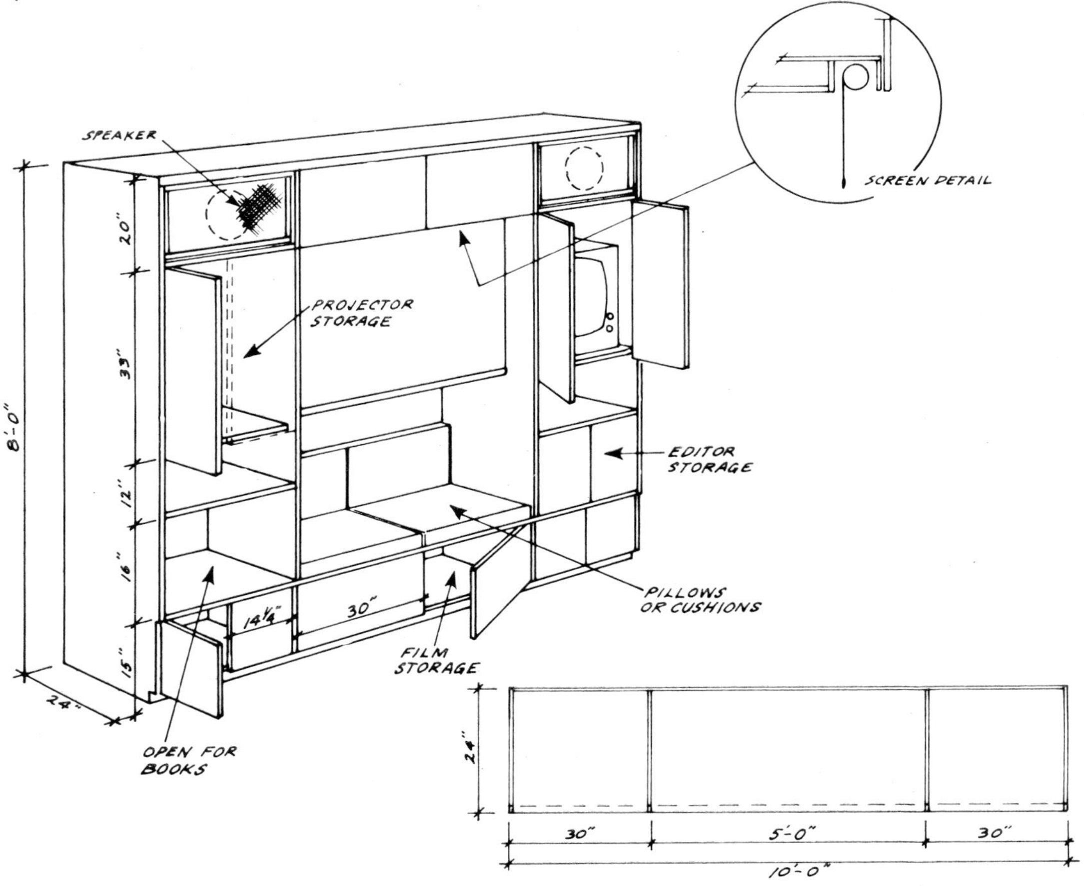

SPEAKER

SCREEN DETAIL

PROJECTOR
STORAGE

20"

33"

8'-0"

12"

16"

15"

24"

14¼"

30"

EDITOR
STORAGE

PILLOWS
OR CUSHIONS

FILM
STORAGE

OPEN FOR
BOOKS

24"

30"

5'-0"

30"

10'-0"

A storage wall designed as an entertainment center
is pictured (opposite page) and explained
in detail sketches (this page). Detail at right, top,
shows construction of the cove housing a movie screen
that pulls down like a window shade. Lower-right
detail gives overall measurements of the unit
as viewed from above. In the photograph, bottom edge
of the screen is visible against the brick wall.
The same unit also holds TV and stereo equipment
with a speaker at either side at the top.
Visible as rectangular screens in the photograph,
speaker openings are covered by fabric in wooden frames.
In addition to space for books, film and projector storage,
there is even room for logs for an adjacent fireplace.
Unit as a whole forms a handsome focal point for the room.
If this particular version doesn't meet your needs,
it's not difficult to design and build one that will.
Consult your local lumber dealer for suggestions,
materials; some dealers will even supply plans.

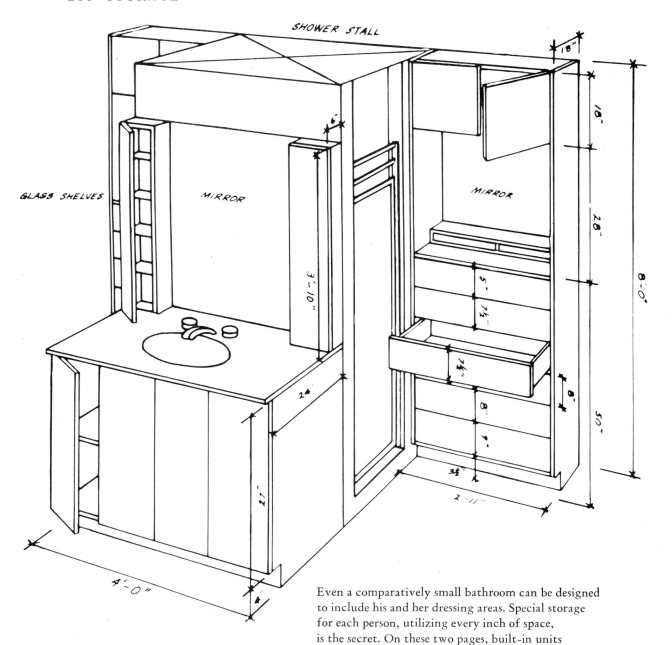

SHOWER STALL

GLASS SHELVES

MIRROR

MIRROR

Even a comparatively small bathroom can be designed
to include his and her dressing areas. Special storage
for each person, utilizing every inch of space,
is the secret. On these two pages, built-in units
with adaptable ideas are detailed in sketch form above
and in the photograph on the facing page.

Here only "her" unit is shown, to the right of the
lavatory; to the left, there is an identical unit for "him."
Adjoining each unit is hanging space (not shown) for clothes.
Directly behind the lavatory is a shower stall;
it could as well be a combination square tub and shower.
Cabinets on either side of the mirror are designed
to store toiletries; space beneath the counter
can be used for towels and other essentials.
In the photograph, a readymade strip
of incandescent lighting has been substituted
for fluorescent strip concealed by cove in the sketch.
Borders around doors and drawers are of decorative braid
applied with a moistureproof adhesive.

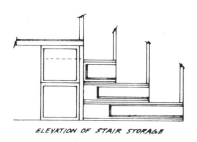

ELEVATION OF STAIR STORAGE

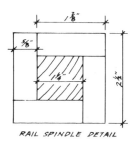

RAIL SPINDLE DETAIL

Room for one—
or two—
to grow in

Coping with the nonstop accumulation by children
of toys, sports gear, and other treasures
presents special problems. Here's one solution—
a nursery with storage designed to grow with the child,
even to make room for another addition to the family.

  The raised platform, with its fence and gate,
needs only a mattress to make it a fine crib.
Space beneath is used as a "garage" for mobile toys.
Drawers for small-toy storage are built into the steps
leading to the crib platform and the supports for it.
Sketch on opposite page shows platform from above;
sketches at left and below, details of construction.

  As the child outgrows a crib, the platform is wide enough
to hold a youth bed. Toy garage could easily accommodate
a trundle bed for another child. Pegboard wall
above the platform might convert to a bulletin board,
shelves holding toys might be used to store books.

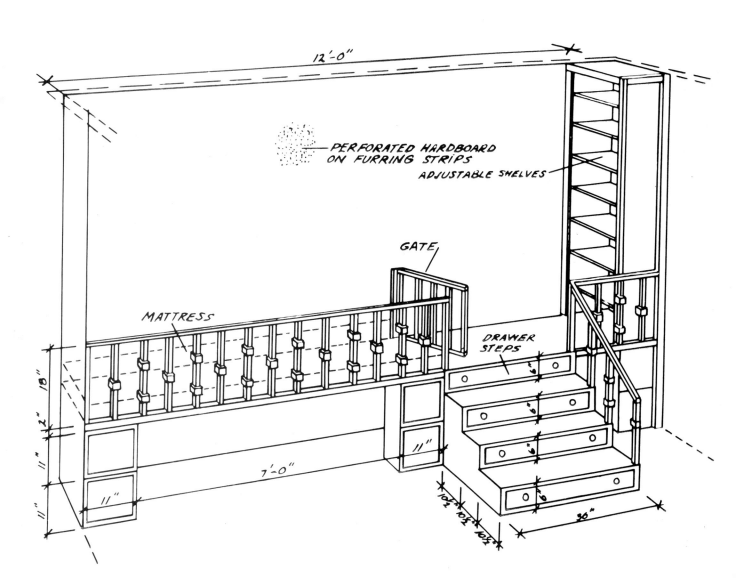

PERFORATED HARDBOARD
ON FURRING STRIPS

ADJUSTABLE SHELVES

GATE

MATTRESS

DRAWER
STEPS

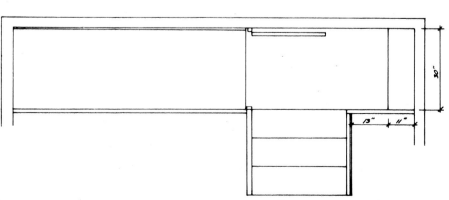

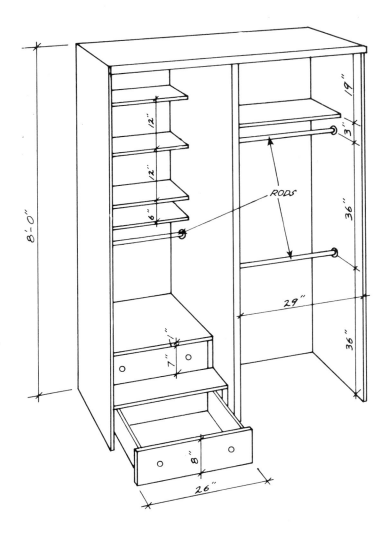

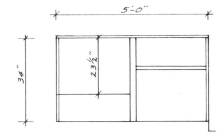

Small fry are more easily enticed into learning to dress themselves if they are able to reach their clothing. Providing steps for that purpose makes the whole thing fun.

The steps here (under the clothes rod at left in both photograph and sketch) lead to the child's everyday clothes. The lowest step is also a deep drawer holding sneakers and other play shoes. Drawer in the second step is used for socks and underthings. Storage bins on shelves above the rod may hold child's out-of-season clothing or the overflow from other closets, all neatly filed for quick retrieval.

Two clothes rods on the right side of the closet hold the balance of the child's wardrobe—choices for him to make on the lower rod, dress-up clothing for Mother to select on the upper one.

The height of the rods can be adjusted as the child grows, the storage shelves removed to make room for an additional rod.

tricks

PROFESSIONAL DECORATORS USE
AND YOU CAN COPY

Decorators, or interior designers as they prefer to be called, do not confine themselves to beautifying duplex apartments on Park Avenue or houses on Nob Hill. Many have clients with limited budgets; others work for department stores or design model homes for housing developments.

As a result, *some* decorator has faced every decorating problem that is likely to occur. In the following pages some of their most ingenious, and most easily adaptable, solutions are shown. In addition, throughout this book and particularly in the next chapter, on do-it-yourself ideas, you'll find other tricks worth copying.

If you are interested in the actual services of a decorator, you will find that many will work on a consultation basis, for an hourly or per diem fee. Others take as their fee the difference between the wholesale cost of any furnishings they buy for the client and the retail price charged her (which is the same price she would pay in the stores). Or they may base their fees not on the purchase of furnishings but on the work involved and the client's budget. Department-store decorators charge a minimum fee or none at all.

In using a decorator's services, make sure you understand before-hand exactly what his—and your—obligations are. The initials AID (American Institute of Interior Designers) or NSID (National Society of Interior Designers) indicate membership in one of two professional societies with high standards for training and experience. However, some good decorators do not belong to either. The best proof of a designer's ability is what he has done. Ask to see photographs, sketches, or, if possible, some completed projects.

Problem: A small apartment living room lacking both drama and room for dining. Solution: One wall is covered with a handsome flocked paper, creating an eyecatching background for shelves. Shirred fabric masks grille-fronted cupboard doors; table projects from wall, serves as a desk as well as for dining.

Problem (opposite): A bedroom with not enough closets.
Solution: Matching wallpaper and fabric were used
to create a sumptuous look, also provide
additional storage space (at head and foot of bed,
cleverly hidden behind fabric shirred
on curtain rods at ceiling height). Other draperies are
supported by provincial-style panels used to frame bed.

Problem (left): A room without architectural interest.
Solution: Wallpaper borders are used to supply a frame
to a frameless window and at the juncture of walls
and ceiling. Borders come readymade in many designs,
from classic architectural moldings, cornices,
and columns to dainty florals and stencil designs.
Or you can use decorative wooden molding, available
from lumber dealers, to achieve a similar effect.

Problem (left): In an open-plan room, separation
was needed between living and dining areas.
Solution: A folding screen neatly does the trick,
while providing a backdrop for the sofa. Screens
are versatile: they may be painted, papered, stenciled,
or covered with fabric in any desired color or design.
Panels are easily hinged together to any width
necessary to hide an awkward or unattractive
architectural element or to create
(and hide) extra storage space.

Problem (left): Not enough seating—and a tight budget.
Solution: A collection of big vinyl-covered cushions,
which may be stacked to seat one or scattered
around the room to accommodate several people.
Pillows are a great favorite with decorators.
Use them to accent or blend with your color scheme,
to add textural interest, to provide design excitement.

Problem (left): An important grouping needed to hang
above a chest. Solution: A mirror and two small
pictures are given the necessary scale and impact
by massive frames. Expensive to buy, frames
of this size can be made inexpensively by mitering
and joining plain wooden boards, then covering them
with vinyl-coated *trompe l'oeil* wallpaper for moiré,
marble, tortoise-shell, many other effects.
(A miter box, available at any hardware store,
makes the job easy.) Or use wooden molding,
which may then be stained, painted, or covered
with fabric, mirror glass, or adhesive-backed plastic.
Another good source for inexpensive frames:
secondhand stores and junkshops; refinish your finds.

Problem (above): A conventional coffee table
might seem dull in this eclectically furnished room.
Solution: An old trunk, scrubbed and varnished,
serves as a handsome and practical substitute,
with the plus of providing extra storage. Other
decorator touches: Screen masks an air conditioner
in the window; louvered shutters substitute for curtains.

Problem (left): Beds lacking headboards. Solution:
Cafe curtains on rods attached to the wall provide
inexpensive finishing touch. Other headboard substitutes:
Wall coverings (vinyl-coated silk, damask, grass cloth),
wallpaper, wood paneling, a wall-hung rug.

Problem (above): A small family room that must serve
several purposes. Solution: Shelves were installed
along one wall to hold TV, tape deck, tuner, records,
other entertainment equipment. Stereo speakers
are above closet doors on either side; folding doors
hide storage wall when equipment is not in use.
Outdoor furniture gives an airy look at low cost;
brick-patterned vinyl tiles match white brick walls.

Problem (right): A breakfast nook to be furnished
for a song. Solution: Refinished table, director's chairs
covered in same fabric as curtains. Readymade covers
come in leather, fake fur, canvas in many colors.

Problem (left and below left): Kitchen lacking a dining area. Solution: Built-in banquettes that offer space-saving comfort as well as extra storage. Here, a U-shaped banquette seats from four to six around a glass-topped table (which also creates an illusion of roominess); long drawers beneath two sides of the banquette store sports equipment. Idea can be adapted to a window seat, which would lift to reveal storage space beneath. The banquette cushions are foam slabs covered with vinyl fabric; the same vinyl tiles used as flooring are also used on the walls.

Problem (below): Bedroom without a center of interest, adequate storage space. Solution: Wooden dowels (available at lumber yards) are used to form the bed's superstructure; a length of fabric, stretched over framework, creates a striking canopy. Drawers beneath bed and chest at foot are used for storage.

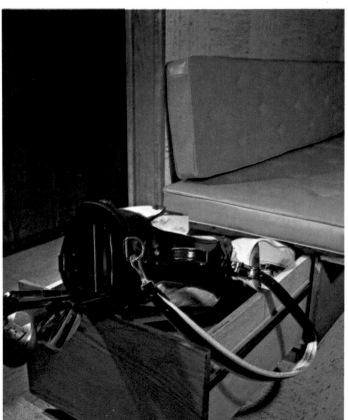

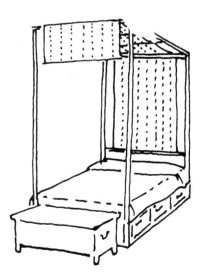

Problem (opposite): Apartment with no space for a study. Solution: Shallow nook formed by jog in the living-room wall is fitted with tension poles that hold a system of shelves, cabinets, drawers, desk space. Grasscloth wall covering is continued over the window valance.

Problem: A game-music room
that must also serve for formal dining
and for entertaining. Solution:
Picture above shows how the game table
is usable for family meals. In picture below,
the drop-leaf study table has been moved
out from the window and its leaves raised
to make room for formal dining.
Sliding plywood panels,
hidden behind painting in top picture,
pull out to cover the book shelves;
chain-hung lighting fixtures, suspended
from hooks in the ceiling, are moved
out of the way of the dining table,
which is illuminated by candles.
Chairs serve equally well in both their roles,
while the tile-patterned vinyl flooring
is as handsome as it is practical.

Problem (above): A small and dreary
foyer. Solution: A handsomely framed
mirror above a narrow shelf
gives an air to the tiniest foyer.
Lighting is provided by a fluorescent
strip behind the wall-hung baffle.
Real marble tile on the floor,
practical for so small an area,
completes the transformation.

Problem (left): Where to put
a home office. Solution: A curved
desk and storage cupboards
are tucked into space beneath
a stairway that would otherwise
be wasted. When the typewriter
is stored away, desk and counter
become a serene continuous shelf
for the display of accessories.
Note too the skillful handling
of the pictures in relation to
the objects in front of them.

Problem (left): Wall space is broken up
by too many doors, giving the room a restless look.
Solution: Paint or paper the doors to match
the walls. When patterned paper is used,
care must be taken to match the design exactly.

Problem (below): The need to tie in a dining room
with the living room from which it is visible.
Solution: The paneled wood walls,
accented by white, of the living room
are effectively counterpointed in the dining room,
where white walls are accented by the wood beams
of the ceiling, the bare wood floor, and the frame
for the window opening (made from the same fabric
used for the upholstery, applied with adhesive).

Problem (above): To show off
an antique French provincial table. Solution:
Painted plank walls, a stylized painting,
brick floor, all combine for a compatible "country" look.

Problem (right): To fill a yawning wall space
behind a sofa. Solution: A handsome wallpaper
was first used to cover the area, stained wood molding
was applied at the sides to define it, and
a well-framed mirror was added to form a focal point.

do-it-yourself

IDEAS FOR EVERY ROOM
IN THE HOUSE

No decorating project offers greater satisfaction than the one you accomplish yourself. It is also true that in this respect some people are more equal than others. The woman with a flair for sewing or needlework and a handyman husband can create effects that make her neighbors despair. On the other hand, there are projects anyone with a little patience can undertake with success.

Paint is the most effective decorating tool known to man—or woman. Don't confine it just to large areas. To accent a particularly handsome piece of furniture, paint the wall behind it a different color from the rest; pick out the molding of a door (or "panel" a flat one); use contrasting colors for the drawers of a chest; paint the shelves of a curio cabinet just the right shade to bring out the beauty of the objects displayed; rescue an old trunk with a coat of varnish.

The new wallpapers and wall coverings are also easy to handle. Many are prepasted or adhesive-backed; you simply dip a strip in water (or peel off the paper backing) and smooth it to the wall. Other materials, such as cork, marble tile, and mirror glass, have a fabric backing to which adhesive may be applied. Some wood paneling can also be applied with adhesive. You can even apply fabric to a wall, although, if the one you choose hasn't been backed for wall application, you may have to stiffen it first with white glue. Glue may stain delicate fabrics such as silk or brocade; stretch these over strips of wood attached to the wall. Though you might not want to tackle a large area in this way, decorative panels can be very effective. Sturdy fabrics like linen or burlap may be tacked or stapled to a wall.

A cheerful—and completely functional—room
designed to keep pace with a growing youngster.
Cabinets and shelves were assembled by the owner;
the desk unit, mounted on brackets fastened to the wall
and to the sturdy easy-to-build ladder,
can be raised in height as the child grows.

Right: Plate glass
to replace battered tabletop
and paint were used to turn
old dining room into new.
Table, chairs, were antiqued,
the table in white, chairs
in green with design details
emphasized with gold.
A sturdy board, covered
in same vinyl used on the floor,
serves as a wall-hung buffet;
the mirror is a junk-shop find
painted to match the chairs.

Left: The same fabric
that covers the couch is used
to rehabilitate an old chest.
Use white glue (or spray
adhesive) and stretch fabric
tight during glueing process;
miter corners for smooth fit.
Before covering drawer fronts,
remove the hardware,
sand to make room for fabric.

Finishing unfinished furniture—readymade or in parts you assemble yourself—or refinishing old pieces, is another rewarding
project. (For books on the subject, see page 243.) With "antiquing"
you can soften the harsh look of a newly painted piece, give a battered
old one new beauty. Often used to "age" furniture, antiquing's decorating possibilities go far beyond that. You can use it to tie a new
piece into an existing color scheme, giving it first a coat of white or a
light color, then toning or shading with a harmonious shade. Or you
can mute a bright color with a darker overtone, letting the vivid
shade peek through here and there. And there is nothing like antiquing to emphasize details of intricate carving or the sculptured relief of

TEXT CONTINUED ON PAGE 234

One-room apartment pictured on these two pages
is full of do-it-yourself ideas. The attractive
and practical window treatment
consists of fretwork panels (available at lumber yards)
framed in wood to add rigidity; small sections
of fretwork are glued to window shades to serve as pulls.
Strip fluorescent lighting, mounted on wall
at ceiling height and concealed by a baffle,
illuminates the desk-dining wall.
One of two studio couches fits neatly
under a corner table designed to serve them both;
at nighttime it rolls out on casters to serve as a bed.
The kind of furniture you buy in parts,
put together yourself to meet your own needs,
makes it easy to solve special problems like this one.

Below: Furniture you assemble yourself is used to create
a nook for writing letters or for reading
or working in comfort. Plastic-laminated tabletop
(laminating kits are available),
fitted with legs on casters is just the right height
for reading, eating, sewing, or watching TV in bed;
the laminated desk unit is wall-mounted. Vertical blinds
control light, unify the corner windows.

Right: Convenience, practicality, and good looks
are all achieved in this custom-planned nursery.
Brackets, mounted on the paint-them-yourself chests,
hold a shelf that can be used now for changing
and dressing the baby, later moved to desk-top height
as he grows. More bracket-mounted shelves hold toys;
the bulletin board is a piece of cork in a wood frame.
Vertical-slat folding door harmonizes with the furniture.

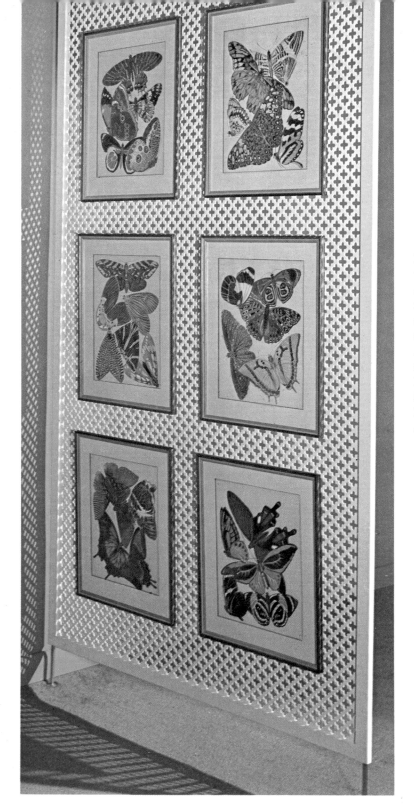

Left: Perforated panel of aluminum,
mounted on floor-to-ceiling tension poles
and hung with framed prints,
makes a handsome and inexpensive
room divider. Other divider ideas:
Wood filigree panels; panels of embossed
translucent plastic, clear, smoked
or tinted; shelves for books or *objets d'arts.*

Right: In-a-wall sewing room designed
to answer every need. Shelves hold boxes
covered with adhesive-backed plastic
for storing fabrics and trimmings;
clear plastic boxes keep thread, needles,
and other findings in plain sight.
Alcove holds finished garments,
also has room for an ironing board.
Knee hole under the sewing-machine table
is backed by a cabinet and drawers;
hinged doors on casters, mirror-paneled
on the inside, swing out to close area off.
(For plans for this unit, see page 244.)

Below: To store items such as placemats
and napkins that get lost in deep drawers,
install wooden guide strips in stock cabinets
to hold shallow shelves that pull out.

raised or molded panels. To make it easy, paint manufacturers offer antiquing kits with all the necessary materials.

To antique furniture, you first apply a coat (two may be necessary) of flat paint, white or a light shade of the finish color. When this has thoroughly dried, a darker paint, or glaze, is put on. This glaze, similar in consistency to finger paint, is allowed to set for a short time, then most of it is wiped off, leaving the darker color in crevices, on edges of panels, or wherever you think is best. It dries slowly, giving you time to experiment. If you don't like the first result, you can wipe it off and start over. Vary the effect by varying the "wipe rag"—use gauze, carpet, burlap, plastic film.

How to "age" furniture

Another technique for "aging" new furniture is called distressing—intentional damage to imitate wear. It is frequently employed on provincial and colonial pieces, using such strange tools as bent wire, an old beer-can opener, a section of tire chain, bent and twisted nails, a chisel with a jagged edge. A look of heavy wear will probably call for a wood rasp or coarse file, used always at random—the same distress mark should not appear twice. You can emphasize distress marks with darker tones of stain or glaze.

Spattering is another good companion to antiquing. Use fine white flecks on a dark surface, dark flecks if the surface is light. Or, to create the impression of wormholes in fruitwood, try black flecks on brown. To spatter, dip bristle tips of a toothbrush or any short, stiff-bristled brush in the paint, then hold it six to nine inches from the surface. Draw a stick, or your thumb, across the bristles; this will cause them to flip back, and fine droplets will spatter onto the surface. It's wise to practice on an old board or piece of paper first.

Stenciling, one of the oldest of American crafts, can create a charming effect not only on furniture but on walls, floors, windowshades, lamps, and other accessories. You can buy stenciling kits (look for them in craft and art supply shops) or make your own design by tracing any pattern that appeals to you and transferring it, via carbon paper, to a sturdy piece of cardboard. Cut out the design, tape the cardboard firmly in position, and brush paint across it. It's best to experiment on a practice surface until you get the hang of the technique and the right paint consistency. After that, it's easy and fun.

In this small fry's retreat, adhesive-backed cork tiles
act as a bulletin board as well as helping
to absorb sound. Another wall is a blackboard;
it can be wiped clean with an eraser.
Brightly painted wooden cubes provide storage for toys,
records, at child's own level; the floor is vinyl.

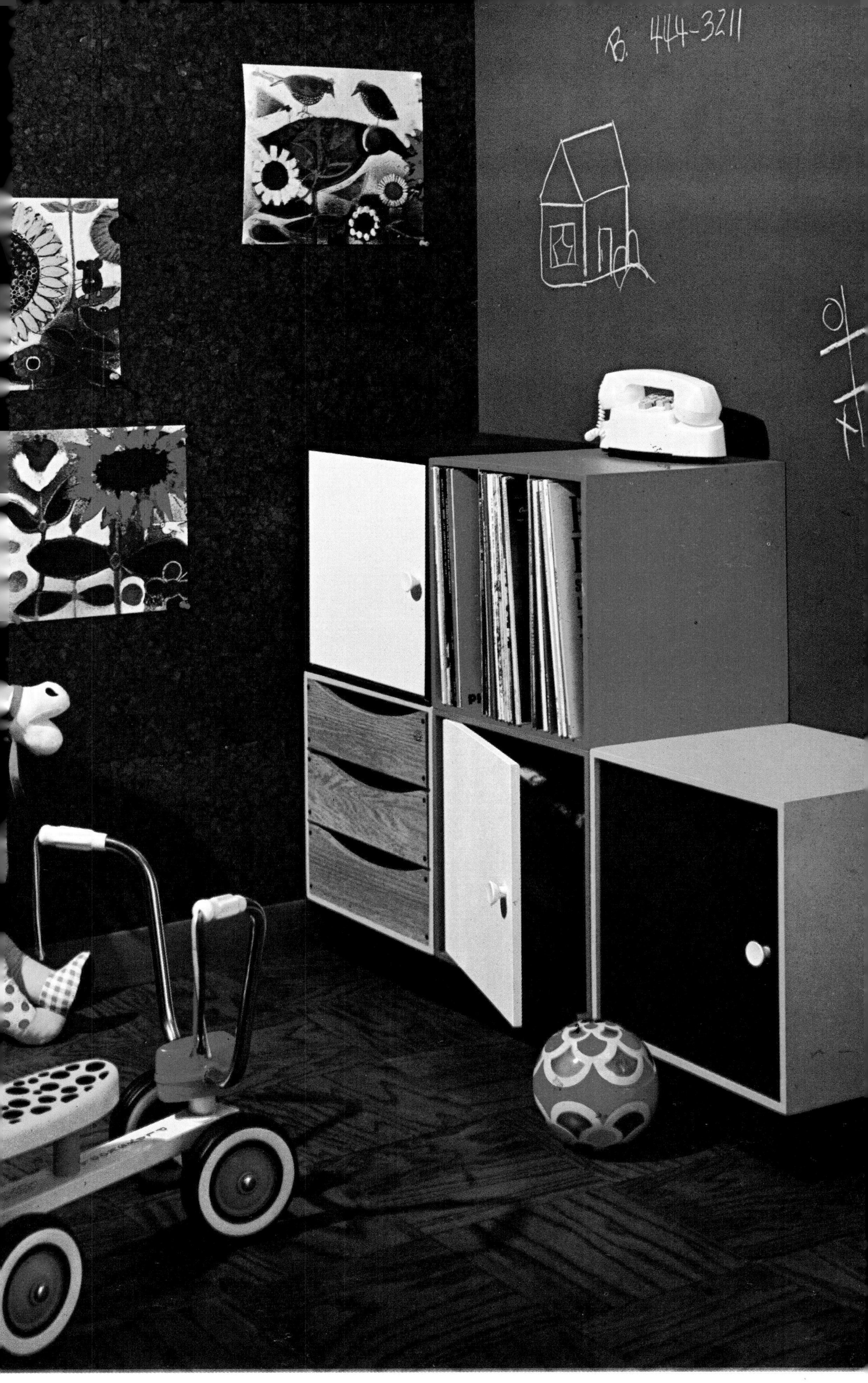
B. 444-3211

Left: Bedroom furniture is enlivened
with a coat of yellow paint, its carving details
highlighted by a contrasting stripe. Blue
of the newly painted wicker chair
repeats dominant color in the wall covering.

Right: In this remodeled attic bathroom,
the plumbing was installed by professionals,
rest of work done by the owners. They built
a washstand cabinet, painted it blue to match
the wall behind it, covered other walls, ceiling,
with wallpaper, and laid the brick-patterned
vinyl floor. Wall-hung shelves, coat rack,
lighting fixtures, and wicker table were found
in a junk shop and repainted; the mirror frame
was refinished and given a gilt border.
Note the skillful use of paint to pick out
architectural details of the room and door.

Products that are a boon to do-it-yourselfers include hardwood,
plywood, and hardboard paneling in many styles and finishes (some
types can be installed with adhesive instead of nails); formica paneling (for bathrooms and kitchens), beams that look as though they
had been taken from an old barn but are made of lightweight
polyurethane; all kinds of wood turnings for posts, bedsteads, balus-
trades; filigree panels of wood, metal, or plastic; wood moldings to
frame doors or windows or create panels or dados on a wall; all kinds
of shelf and wall systems to be assembled and finished as desired;
adhesive-backed plastic in a vast range of colors and patterns; iron-on
laminating shade cloth; adhesive glue in a spray can (use it to
laminate fabric onto walls, mirror frames), kits for resurfacing with
plastic laminates. And don't forget the treasures to be found in
antique or junk shops—or in your own attic or basement. An old tray
may make a unique tabletop, a tarnished mirror supply a frame for a
picture. Try decoupage on a battered chest or a humble tin box to
make it look like a collector's item.

Above: Stock plywood cabinets are given a new look
when doors are stained and finished with a sealer,
frames painted a deep pink for contrast.
Easily laid ceramic tile is used for countertops;
brick-patterned vinyl wall covering is scrubbable.

Opposite: With a little practice, stenciling,
one of the oldest American decorating crafts,
goes quickly. In this room with a Colonial air,
the soft blue walls are stenciled
with a simple design in a deeper shade of blue
to emphasize the room's architectural features.
The draped valance is typical of the period.

Left: To redo an old chest or dress up a new one, try borrowing a fabric pattern for its decoration. First trace the pattern on tissue paper, then transfer it to the chest with carbon paper. Use oil paints to color the design; let it dry thoroughly and finish off with a clear sealer coat.

Center: For a striking set of nesting tables, cover one with a patterned adhesive-backed plastic; use solid colors in the pattern for the other two. Adhesive-backed plastic comes in a great variety of patterns and colors, and can be used to cover almost any surface.

Bottom: Wooden cubes, open on one side, are useful for tables, for extra seating, and/or for storage. Make them yourself or buy them unfinished and paint or cover them. Those pictured are covered with adhesive-backed vinyl floor tiles—you simply cut tiles to fit (use scissors), peel off the protective paper and apply them. Or use adhesive-backed plastic.

Right: An old sideboard and shelf are given new life by a coat of paint, an antique glaze finish, and stencil motifs that continue up the wall to emphasize the grouping. Designs and all materials for stenciling come in kits; look for them in art supply, craft, and hardware stores.

appendix

PLACES TO VISIT

BOOKS FOR FURTHER READING

PLACES TO VISIT

Alabama: The Bellingrath Home, near Mobile
California: The Larkin House, Monterey
Connecticut: Old Stone House, Guilford;
Buttolph-Williams House, Wethersfield
Hempsted House, New London
The Joseph Webb House, Wethersfield
Litchfield Village, Litchfield
Delaware: Winterthur, Wilmington
Amstel House, New Castle
Old Dutch House, New Castle
District of Columbia: White House, Washington
The Octagon (James Madison Home), Washington
Florida: "The Oldest House," Saint Augustine
Arrivas House, Saint Augustine
Georgia: Historic District, Savannah
Illinois: Thorne Model Rooms, Chicago Art Institute
Indiana: J. F. D. Lanier Mansion, Madison
Louisiana: Shadows-on-the-Teche, New Iberia
French Quarter, New Orleans
Maine:
The Tate House, Portland
Sweat Mansion, Portland
Victoria Mansion, Portland
Lady Pepperell Mansion, Kittery Point

Maryland: Hammond-Harwood House, Annapolis
Massachusetts: Fairbanks Homestead, Dedham
Old Deerfield Village, Deerfield
Adams Birthplace, Quincy
Harrison Gray Otis House, Boston
House of Seven Gables, Salem
Derby Mansion, Salem
Pingree House, Salem
Michigan: Henry Ford Museum, Dearborn
Mississippi: "Rosalie," Natchez
Connelly's Tavern, Natchez
New Hampshire: Garrison House, Exeter
MacPhedris-Warner House, Portsmouth
New Mexico: Palace of the Governors, Santa Fe
New York: Cooper-Hewitt Museum of Decorative Arts and Design, Smithsonian Institution
American Wing of the Metropolitan Museum, New York City
The Frick Mansion, New York City
The Morris-Jumel Mansion, New York City
Corning Glass Museum, Corning
Brooklyn Museum, Brooklyn
Munson-William Proctor (House and Museum), Rochester

Boscobel, Garrison
Schuyler Mansion, Albany
Hasbrouck House, New Paltz
North Carolina: Tryon Palace, New Bern
Old Salem, Winston-Salem
Ohio: The Taft Museum, Cincinnati
Adena, Chillicothe
The Hale Farm and Village, Akron
Pennsylvania: Rock Ford House, Lancaster
Wheatland, Lancaster
Powel House, Philadelphia
Houses in Fairmount Park, Philadelphia
Rhode Island: Historic District, Newport
South Carolina: Historic District, Charleston
Tennessee: The Hermitage, Nashville
Texas: Governor's Palace, San Antonio
Vermont: Shelburne Museum, Shelburne
Virginia: Williamsburg Restorations, Williamsburg
Gunston Hall, near Alexandria
Stratford Hall, Westmoreland County, Lerty
Adam Thoroughgood House, Virginia Beach, east of Norfolk
Monticello, Charlottesville
Mount Vernon, Fairfax County, near Alexandria

BOOKS FOR FURTHER READING

Aaronson, Joseph. *New Encyclopedia of Furniture.* New York: Crown Publishers, Inc., 1967.

Bergen, John. *All about Upholstering.* New York: Hawthorn Books, 1962.

Boger, Louise Ade and Boger, H. Batterson, *Dictionary of Antiques and the Decorative Arts.* New York: Charles Scribner's Sons, 1957.

Chaffers, William. *Collector's Handbook of Marks and Monograms on Pottery and Porcelain.* New York: Dover Publications, Inc., 1968.

Dal Fabbro, Mario. *How to Make Built-in Furniture.* New York: F. W. Dodge Corp., 1955.

Drepperd, Carl W. *First Reader for Antique Collectors.* New York: Doubleday & Company, Inc., 1948.

Greer, Michael. *Inside Design.* New York: Doubleday & Company, Inc., 1962.

Grotz, George. *Furniture Doctor.* New York: Doubleday & Company, Inc., 1962.

Guild, Vera P. *Good Housekeeping New Complete Book of Needlecraft.* New York: Good Housekeeping Books, 1971.

Lee, Doris and Blanch, Arnold. *Painting for Enjoyment.* New York: Tudor Publishing Co., 1947.

Lee, Ruth. *Exploring the World of Pottery.* Chicago: Children's Press, 1967.

Loria, Jeffry H. *Collecting Original Art.* New York and London: Harper & Row, 1965.

McKearin, George S. and Helen. *American Glass.* New York: Crown Publishers, Inc., 1948.

Mikesell, Arthur M. *The Popular Mechanics Home Book of Refinishing Furniture.* New York: Hawthorn Books, 1966.

Nutting, Wallace. *Furniture Treasury.* New York: The Macmillan Company, 1954.

Pahlmann, William. *Pahlmann Book of Interior Design.* New York: The Viking Press, Inc., 1968.

Reif, Rita. *Treasure Rooms of America's Mansions, Manors and Houses.* New York: Coward-McCann, Inc., 1970.

Roberts, Patricia Easterbrook. *Table Settings, Entertaining and Etiquette.* New York: The Viking Press, Inc., 1967.

Varney, Carleton, *You and Your Apartment.* The Bobbs-Merrill Co., Inc., 1968.

Waring, Janet. *Early American Stencils.* New York: Dover Publications, Inc., 1968.

Williams, Henry Lionel and Ottalie K. *A Treasury of Great American Houses.* New York, G. P. Putnam's Sons, 1970.

Winchester, Alice, and Antiques Magazine. *Antiques Treasury of Furniture and Decorative Arts.* New York, E. P. Dutton & Co., Inc., 1959.

Wyler, Seymour B. *Book of Old Silver.* New York: Crown Publishers, Inc., 1937.

INTERIOR DESIGNERS' CREDITS

Allen, Mrs. Sydney, NSID: page 157. *Barrett, David, AID:* pages 46–47, 117, 158, 213. *Bell, David Eugene, AID:* page 42. *Berman, Samson, AID & Associates:* pages 140, 203, 221, 225, 230. *Beukema, Fred:* pages 23, 168. *Bieger, Louise, AID:* pages 80, 87, 101, 182–183, 193, 236. *Bowman, William, Inc.:* page 67. *Brunelle, Charles B.:* pages 113, 174. *Butler, Richard, AID:* pages 50–51. *Catterton, Blair, AID:* pages 53, 175. *D'Arcy, Barbara, AID:* pages 14, 71, 72, 109. *Erb, Catherine:* pages 220, 222. *Feray, Irene, AID:* pages 29, 172, 185. *Gasperecz, Stephen, AID:* page 163. *Gilmore, David:* pages 43, 199. *Glaser, Don, AID:* pages 63, 132, 134. *Gordon, Olga:* pages 57, 105, 177. *Himmel, Richard, AID:* pages 32, 48, 54, 205, 207, 209, 217, 218, 238. *Holtz, Harold, AID:* pages 77, 103. *Kelly, Virginia Whitmore, AID:* page 131. *Kettering, Paul, AID:* pages 58–59, 114, 171, 211. *Lincoln, Frank J. Jr., AID:* pages 49, 55, 69 (top right), 107, 160. *Lumsden, James:* pages 74–75. *Malino, Emily, AID:* page 219. *Marchetti, Stephen:* page 215. *McCarty, Jim, AID:* page 143. *Milam, Hank:* pages 74–75. *Morse, James Childs, AID:* page 119. *Motyka, Edmund, AID:* pages 27, 125, 227. *Murray, Charles, AID:* pages 44, 45, 79, 147. *Paul, Dorothy, AID:* page 69 (bottom left). *Piner, Duke, AID:* page 124. *Reitz, Beverly, AID:* page 155. *Rothberg, Howard P.:* page 223. *Schneider, Robert L.:* pages 82–83. *Shrallow, Fred, AID:* pages 159, 228–229, 231. *Smith, Ving, AID* and *Charlotte:* page 22. *Squire, Staniford, AID:* page 162. *Stephenson, Olive, AID,* and *Eugene, FAID:* pages: 129, 130, 133, 149, 169. *Targer, Scott:* pages 16, 150. *Thomas, Mr. and Mrs. Jack, AID:* page 35. *Tregre, Louis, AID:* page 191. *Weyerhauser Corporation:* pages 204, 206, 208, 210

PHOTOGRAPHERS' CREDITS

Alderman Studios: pages 92, 151, 168, 178, 239. *Balz, Wesley:* pages 60–61, 121, 233, 235. *Bourdon, Edward A.:* pages 43, 199. *Bruton, Bill:* pages 41, 68, 97, 111. *DeEvia, Edgar:* pages 11, 13, 30, 108, 187, 189, 190, 191, 192, 195, 197. *Fenn, Otto:* pages 53, 175, 179. *Gibbardt, Harold:* pages 126, 127. *Graff, Howard:* pages 18–19, 20, 31, 32, 46–47, 48, 54, 70, 81, 117, 139, 155, 158, 167, 173, 176, 181, 184, 202, 205, 207, 209, 211, 213, 217, 218, 232, 238. *Howland Associates:* page 223. *Jarrett, Bill:* pages 23, 73. *Lisanti, Vincent:* pages 58–59, 83, 114, 171. *Margerin, Bill:* pages 89, 137, 153, 237. *Roedel, O. Philip:* pages 8, 14, 16, 17, 22, 27, 28, 29, 33, 35, 44, 45, 57, 63, 71, 72, 79, 85, 90, 93, 95, 105, 109, 113, 119, 122, 123, 124, 125, 129, 130, 131, 132, 133, 134, 138, 140, 141, 143, 145, 146, 147, 150, 157, 159, 160, 162, 163, 172, 174, 177, 185, 194, 201, 203, 215, 216, 219, 220, 221, 225, 230, 231. *Silva, Ernest M.:* pages 42, 49, 50–51, 55, 107, 135, 136, 149, 154, 169, 226, 227, 228–229, 240, 241. *Szanik, George R.:* pages 67, 69, 74–75, 80, 87, 101, 182–183, 193, 236. *Ward, Nowell Associates:* page 56. *Zimmerman, Don:* pages 24–25, 77, 103.

OTHER CREDITS

The Color and Pattern and Texture Charts on pages 36–39 and 64–65 have been adapted, by permission, from the booklet *Color, Texture and Design in Space,* copyright © 1968 by The Sperry and Hutchinson Company.

For the plans for the In-a-Wall Sewing Room shown on page 233, send 35¢ (in coin, check, or money order) to: Good Housekeeping Bulletin Service, 959 Eighth Avenue, New York, N.Y. 10019.

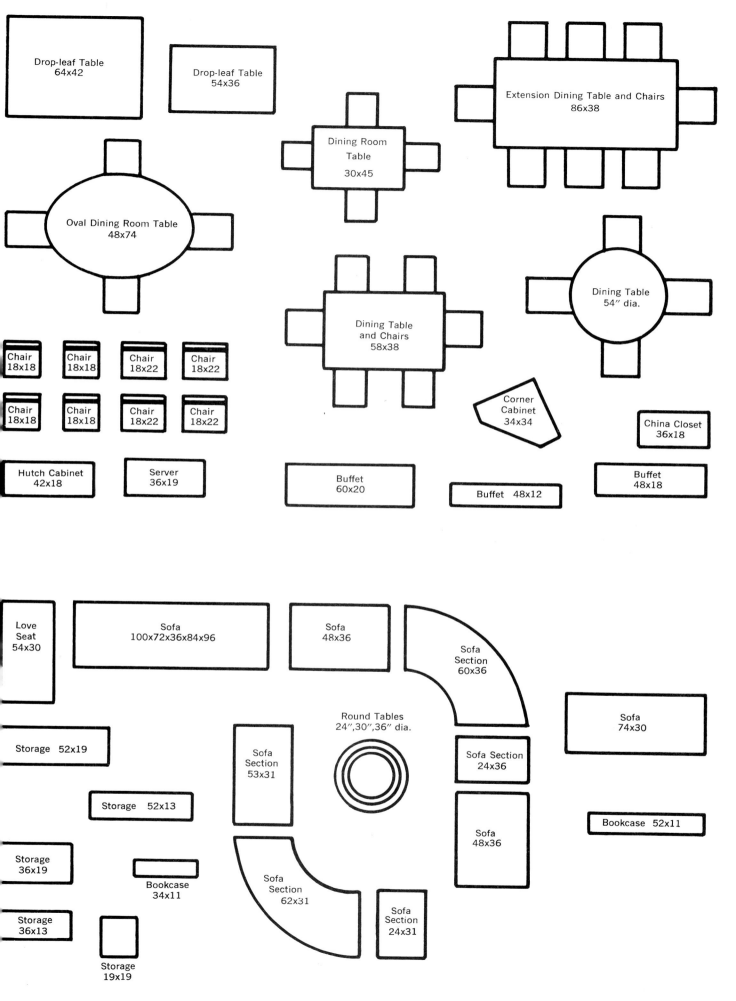

Drop-leaf Table
64x42

Drop-leaf Table
54x36

Extension Dining Table and Chairs
86x38

Dining Room
Table
30x45

Oval Dining Room Table
48x74

Dining Table
54" dia.

Chair
18x18

Chair
18x18

Chair
18x22

Chair
18x22

Chair
18x18

Chair
18x18

Chair
18x22

Chair
18x22

Dining Table
and Chairs
58x38

Corner
Cabinet
34x34

China Closet
36x18

Hutch Cabinet
42x18

Server
36x19

Buffet
60x20

Buffet 48x12

Buffet
48x18

Love
Seat
54x30

Sofa
100x72x36x84x96

Sofa
48x36

Sofa
Section
60x36

Sofa
74x30

Storage 52x19

Round Tables
24",30",36" dia.

Sofa
Section
53x31

Sofa Section
24x36

Storage 52x13

Sofa
48x36

Bookcase 52x11

Storage
36x19

Bookcase
34x11

Sofa
Section
62x31

Sofa
Section
24x31

Storage
36x13

Storage
19x19

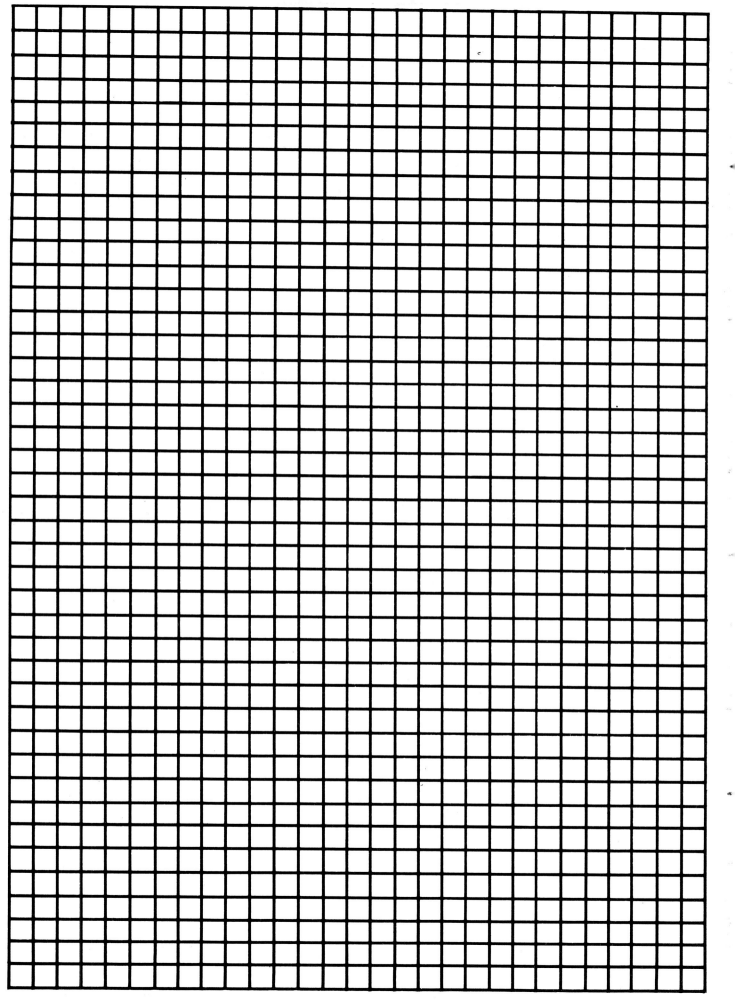

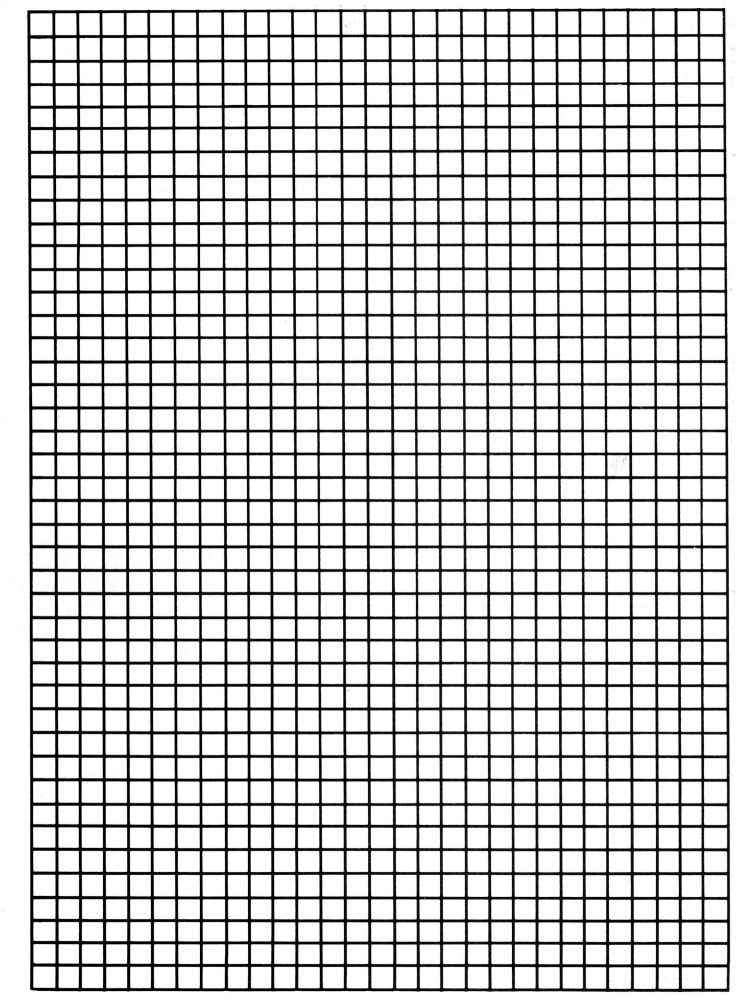

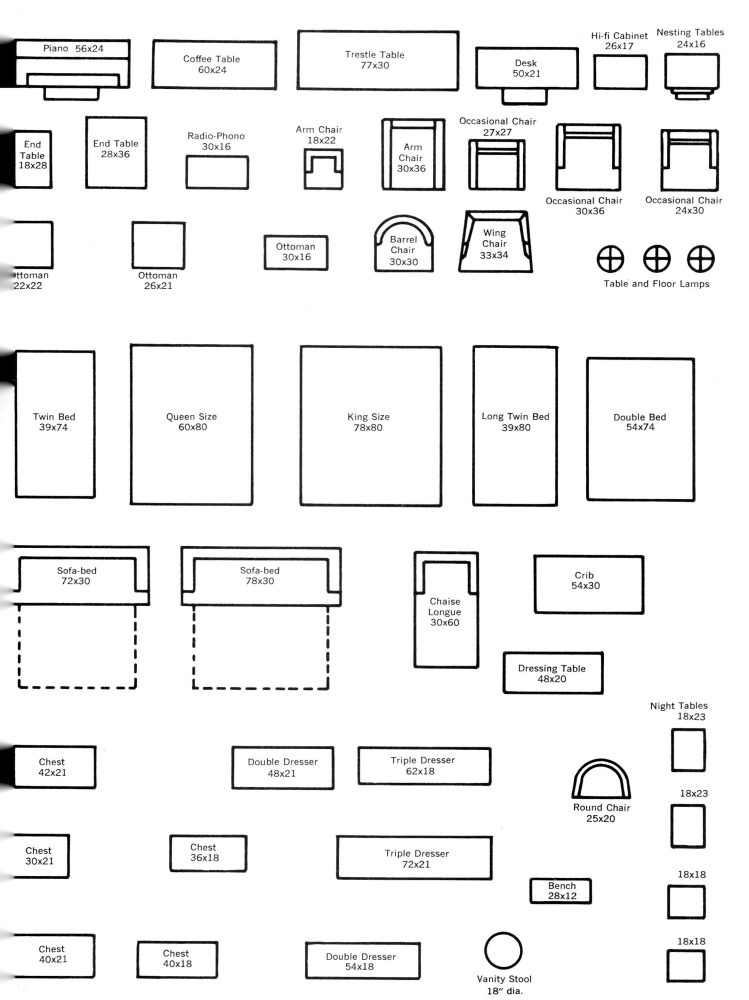

Piano 56x24

Coffee Table
60x24

Trestle Table
77x30

Desk
50x21

Hi-fi Cabinet
26x17

Nesting Tables
24x16

End
Table
18x28

End Table
28x36

Radio-Phono
30x16

Arm Chair
18x22

Arm
Chair
30x36

Occasional Chair
27x27

Occasional Chair
30x36

Occasional Chair
24x30

Ottoman
22x22

Ottoman
26x21

Ottoman
30x16

Barrel
Chair
30x30

Wing
Chair
33x34

Table and Floor Lamps

Twin Bed
39x74

Queen Size
60x80

King Size
78x80

Long Twin Bed
39x80

Double Bed
54x74

Sofa-bed
72x30

Sofa-bed
78x30

Chaise
Longue
30x60

Crib
54x30

Dressing Table
48x20

Night Tables
18x23

Chest
42x21

Double Dresser
48x21

Triple Dresser
62x18

Round Chair
25x20

18x23

Chest
30x21

Chest
36x18

Triple Dresser
72x21

18x18

Bench
28x12

Chest
40x21

Chest
40x18

Double Dresser
54x18

Vanity Stool
18" dia.

18x18

Index

Page numbers in italics refer to captions for illustrations

Accessories, *81*, *166*, *168*, *174*, *175*, *176*
  arranging, *170*, *172*
  bathroom, *180*, *182*, *183*
  bedroom, *180*
  color schemes and, *42*, *43*, *170*
  create your own, *170*
  dining room, *170*, *176*, *180*
  finding, *166*, *168*
  flowers as, *12*, *42*, *170*, *185*, *192*, *194*
  kitchen, *16*, *180*, *184*
  living room, *30*, *169*, *172*, *173–74*, *176*, *177*, *178*
  plants as, *79*, *151*, *157*, *166*, *170*, *178*, *180*, *185*
  for pleasure, *166*
  in table settings, *192*, *194*, *199*
  useful, *166*
  See also Mantels; Pictures; individual accessories

Adam brothers furniture, *99*
African influence on color, *54*
American Empire style, *100*
American Institute of Interior Designers (AID), *212*
Antiques, *10*, *23*, *32*, *72*, *89*, *96*, *102*, *175*, *176*, *178*, *186*, *202*
  searching for, *26*
Apartment
  living room, *12*, *21*, *125*, *212*
  one-room, *228*
  study, *218*
Asphalt tile flooring, *86*
Attic, remodeling, *22*, *28*, *236*
Aubusson rug, *92*

Banquettes, *218*
Basement, remodeling, *22*
Bathrooms, *56*, *236*
  accessories for, *180*, *182*, *183*
  carpets and rugs for, *56*, *180*, *182*
  lighting for, *56*, *137*, *180*, *183*, *206*, *237*
  storage in, *206*
Bedrooms, *28*, *48*, *68*, *72*, *108*, *118*, *149*, *214*, *218*, *236*
  accessories for, *180*
  child's, *118*, *210*, *224*, *234*
  lighting for, *132*, *134*, *138*, *140*
  planning, *116*, *118*
Beds, *118*, *216*, *218*
  brass canopy, *108*
  refinished, *108*
  See also Sofas, bed
Bedspreads, *72*, *180*

Biedermeier style, *21*, *100*
Blinds
  rollup matchstick, *83*
  split bamboo, *62*, *162*, *164*
  Venetian, *81*, *154*, *156*, *158*, *162*, *230*
Book
  cases, *127*, *202*
  shelves, *25*, *125*, *174*
Breakfast areas, *32*, *150*, *217*
Brick
  fireplaces, *19*, *66*, *67*, *75*
  flooring, *78*, *80*, *91*, *223*
  walls, *16*, *62*, *66*, *217*

Cabinets, *72*, *163*, *170*, *238*
  kitchen, *84*
Candlesticks
  brass, *10*, *175*
  crystal, *133*
  silver, *191*
Cane
  for furniture, *72*, *98*, *101*
  texture of, *72*
Carpets, *78*, *86*, *94*
  of acrylic fibers, *89*, *91*
  bathroom, *56*
  and color schemes, *86*, *88*
  colors of, *86*, *88*

  cut pile, *88*
  high-low loop, *88*
  indoor-outdoor, *91*
  kitchen, *91–92*
  of nylon fibers, *89*, *91*
  of nylon/polyester fiber, *91*
  padding for, *91*
  of polyester fibers, *91*
  of polypropylene fibers, *91*
  price of, *91*, *94*
  random-sheared, *88*
  shag, *72*, *86*, *88*
  single-level-loop, *88*
  squares, self-adhesive, *94*
  textures and patterns in, *88*
  tip-sheared, *88*
  twist, *88*
  velvet, *88*
  of wool fibers, *88–89*, *91*.
  See also Rugs
Ceilings
  color and, *42*
  luminous, *137*, *140*
  rugs and, *72*
  stained beams, *57*, *222*
  wallpaper and, *76*
Chairs
  American Empire, *100*
  antiqued, *226*
  banister-back, *10*
  bentwood, *192*
  chart of styles, *98–100*
  Chinese design, *40*
  Chippendale, *99*
  director's, *217*
  Duncan Phyfe, *100*
  early American, *99*
  early English, *98*
  English Regency, *100*
  French Empire, *100*
  French provincial, *23*, *99*
  Hepplewhite, *99*
  Hitchcock, *96*
  Italian, *98*
  Louis XIV, *98*
  Louis XV, *34*, *98*

Louis XVI, 98, 152
modern, 100
plastic-framed, 104
Queen Anne, 96, 98
seats, caned, 72, 101
Sheraton, 99
slipcovers for, 102, 108
upholstered, 102, 104
Victorian, 100
wicker, 236
Windsor, 96, 99
Chandeliers. See Lighting, permanent
Chart of furniture styles, 98–100
Chests, 68, 101, 111, 118, 202, 226
   Chinese 40
   construction of, 110–11
   to redo, 240
   spice, 96
Chinese designs, 40, 190
Chippendale furniture, 56, 89, 99
Clocks, 81, 178
   antique, 32
   pillar-and-scroll, 10
Colonial American style, 71, 89, 99, 141
Color, 32, 34–61
   African influence on, 54
   cool, 37, 40
   early American style and, 54
   effect of light on, 34, 37, 39, 40, 128
   French provincial style and, 56
   Georgian style and, 56, 61
   hues, 36, 37
   intensity, 36, 37, 38, 42
   Louis XV and XVI styles and, 54, 56
   modern style and, 61
   nature and, 40
   neutrals, 36
   Oriental influence on, 54
   Regency style and, 61
   shades, 36
   textures and, 44, 65
   tints, 36
   used by earlier civilizations, 54
   value, 36, 37, 38, 42
   Victorian style and, 61
   warm, 37, 40
   wheel, 36
   wood as a, 44, 48
   See also Color schemes
Color schemes, 23, 27, 34, 40, 42, 43, 48, 49, 50, 53, 55, 58, 94, 170
   choosing, 42–44, 48, 52
   climate and, 40
   color-flow plan, 44, 52, 54
   colors affect one another, 39
   complementary, 38, 42
   cool colors, 38–39, 57
   fads in, 44
   necessity of major color in, 42–44, 52, 54
   one-color (monochromatic), 38, 42, 43–44
   related (analogous), 38, 42
   room exposure and, 40
   and room proportions, 42
   and room size, 40, 42
   rugs and carpets in, 46, 86, 88
   warm colors, 38–39
   See also Color
Concrete flooring, 81
Corduroy for upholstery, 106
Cotton
   for draperies, 148
   for rugs, 74
   texture of, 65, 66
   for upholstery, 106
Couches, studio, 228
   See also Sofas
Cubes, 51, 103, 240

Cupboards, 68, 174, 202, 212
   beneath stairway, 221
   corner, 176
   hutch, 96, 175
Curtains, 12, 150, 152, 164
   cafe, 32, 84, 150, 152, 158, 159, 161, 164, 216
   casement, 150, 159
   for entire wall, 144, 155
   glass, 150
   hardware for hanging, 32, 152, 154, 156, 158, 159, 164

measuring for, 165
ruffled, 150, 164
shower, 180, 182
tailored, 150
valances for, 150, 164
See also Draperies

Decorating schemes
   cost of, 15
   for day-to-day living, 10, 15
   mixing periods in, 22
   need of privacy in, 10
   needs of family considered in, 10
   response to life styles in, 16, 21–23
   rules for, 10
Decorators, 212
   tricks used by, 212, 214–23
Deerfield Museum, 21
Designs. See Patterns
Desks, 178, 212
   child's, 224

curved, 221
drop-front Chippendale, 89
dropleaf, 118
rustic, 141
school, 19
writing, 152
Dining rooms, 23, 42, 51, 62, 71, 79, 81, 83, 92, 186, 197, 199, 220, 222, 226
   accessories, 170, 176, 180
   lighting, 51, 133–34, 186
   nook, 120, 125
   planning, 116

Dinnerware, 186, 190
  china (porcelain), 186, 188, 190
    bone, 188
    decoration on, 188
      overglaze, 188
      underglaze, 188
    earthenware (pottery), 188
      stoneware or ironstone, 175, 188
    glass-ceramic, 188
    melamine, 188
    open stock, 190
Directoire style, 92, 130
Do-it-yourself ideas, 224–40
  products for, 236, 240
  See also Furniture, refinishing; individual methods, products, etc.

Draperies, 32, 118, 146, 148, 149, 161, 164
  cornices and valances for, 149, 154, 161, 164, 238
  fabrics for, 146
    colorfastness to light, 146
    cotton, 148
    fiber glass, 146, 148
    linen, 148
    polyester fibers, 148
    silk, 148
  hardware for hanging, 152, 154, 156, 164
  linings, 149
  making your own, 152, 165
  measuring for, 165
  See also Curtains

Early American style, 21, 91, 96, 99, 141, 146, 166, 172, 173, 188
  braided rugs for, 94
  colors of, 54
  hearth tools, 176
  kitchen, 16, 184
Early English style, 98, 124
English Regency style, 100, 130
  colors of, 61
Étagères, 80, 120, 123

Fabrics
  colorfast, 108
  for curtains, 150, 152
  for draperies, 146
  for slipcovers, 108
  stain-resistant finish on, 108
  texture in, 65, 66, 68, 72
  trimmings on, 72
  for upholstery, 102, 104–8
  uses of, 68, 79
  for wall coverings, 15, 72, 224
  See also individual fabrics
Family rooms, 19, 22, 28, 54, 60, 75, 101, 104, 138, 192, 194, 202, 217
Federal style, 100
Fiber glass draperies, 146, 148
Fireplaces, 67, 75
  brick wall, 19, 66
  hearth tools for, 176
  See also Mantels
Flagstone flooring, 78, 80, 83
Flatware, 186, 188, 191
  hollowware, 192
  serving pieces, 192
  silver plate, 192
  stainless steel, 188, 192
  sterling silver, 191
  vermeil, 192
Flooring, hard-surface, 78, 94
  man-made, 81, 84, 86
  natural, 78, 80–81, 81, 91
  texture in, 66
  See also individual materials
Floors, 78–94
  See also Carpets; Flooring; Rugs
Flowers, 12, 42, 170, 185, 192, 194

Foyers, 79, 221
French doors, 164
French Empire style, 22, 100, 158
French provincial style, 15, 23, 49, 76, 78, 99, 188, 223
  colors of, 56
Fruitwoods, furniture of, 99
Furniture, 96–111
  arrangement of, 112, 116, 120
  chart of, 98–100
  construction of, 106, 110–11
  mixing styles, 102
  outdoor, 217
  period adaptations, 102
  plastic, 110
  refinishing, 108, 226
    antiquing, 226, 234
    distressing, 234
    spattering, 234
    stenciling, 234
  selecting, 96
  traditional vs. modern, 96, 102
  unassembled, 228, 230
  unfinished, 108, 226
  upholstered, 102, 104–8
    colorfast, 108
    construction of, 104
    fabrics for, 102, 104–8
    filling and padding for, 104
    slipcovers for, 102, 108
    stain-resistant finish on, 108
  wood, 102, 108
    distressed, 110
    plastic-laminate tops on, 110
    substitutes, 110
    veneers, 108, 110
  See also Antiques; individual styles and kinds

Georgian style, 99
  colors of, 56, 61
Glassware, 186, 188, 192
  colored, 194
  crystal, 192
  cut, 195
  hand-blown, 194
  pressed, 194

Good Housekeeping New Complete Book of Needlecraft, 94, 152

Headboards, 48, 68, 72
Hepplewhite furniture, 56, 99
Hitchcock chair, 96
Home offices, 221

Italian style, 98

Jacobean style, 98

Kitchens, 60, 84, 159, 218
  accessories, 16, 180, 184
  carpets, 91–92
  lighting for, 60, 140
  planning, 120, 122

Lamps, 72, 101, 130, 132, 173,
    178, 220
  bedside, 132
  candlestick, 141
  ceramic, 80, 172
  column, 130
  converted from candelabra, 25
  converted oil lamps, 128
  cylinder, 138
  figure, 134, 141
  glass, 21
  jar, 141
  Oriental design, 106
  pole, 54
  rooster, 150
  shades, 72, 128, 132, 133, 141,
    142, 178
  urn-shaped, 181
  vase, 133
  vigil lights, 134
  wall-hung, 125, 132
  See also Light; Lighting
Lawson sofa, 91
Light, 129–41
  artificial, 37
  color, effect on, 34, 37, 39, 128

natural, 37, 138
reflecting quality of, 34, 40,
    128
texture and, 44, 62, 65
See also Lamps; Lighting

Lighting
  accent, 128, 130, 138, 228
  architectural, 128, 130
  artificial, 37, 128, 157
  background, 128, 130
  bathroom, 56, 137, 180, 183,
    206, 236
  bedroom, 132, 134, 138, 140
  children's rooms, 140
  dimmer systems, 130, 133,
    134
  dining room, 51, 133–134,
    186
  direct, 130
  incandescent vs. fluorescent,
    140
  kitchen, 60, 140
  living room, 132–33, 134
  permanent, 25, 113, 125, 128,
    130, 133, 138, 140
  portable, 128
  strip, 130, 134, 137, 140, 221,
    228
  work areas, 140
  See also Lamps; Light
Linen
  for draperies, 148
  texture of, 66
Linoleum, 32, 84, 86
Living rooms, 10, 12, 15, 21, 25,
    44, 51, 53, 57, 58, 75,
    80, 83, 86, 89, 112, 123,
    124, 125, 130, 190, 191,
    202, 212, 222
  accessories for, 30, 169, 172,
    173–74, 176, 177, 178
  lighting, 132–33, 134
  planning, 112, 115, 116, 120
Louis XIII style, 98
Louis XIV style, 98

Louis XV style, 21, 34, 98
  colors of, 54, 56
Louis XVI style, 98, 152
  colors of, 53, 56

Mahogany furniture, 99, 100
Mantels, decoration on, 10, 25,
    120, 128, 172, 174, 175,
    176
Marble flooring, 78, 221
Masonry on walls, 66
Mirrors, 21, 34, 137, 183, 214,
    221, 223, 226, 236
  panels, 156, 157
Modern style, 16, 21, 28, 32, 42,
    57, 86, 100, 101, 104,
    106, 123, 130, 161, 177,
    190
  colors of, 61
  vs. traditional, 96, 102

National Society of Interior Designers (NSID), 212
Nature
  and color association, 40
  learning from, in decorating,
    26
Needlepoint, 178
  rugs, 94
Nurseries, 230
  storage in, 208

Oak furniture, 98
Organdy, texture of, 65
Oriental rugs. *See* Rugs, Oriental
Oriental style, 106, 141
  influence on color, 54
  See also Chinese design

Paint
  for decorating, 224
  textured, 66
Paintings. *See* Pictures
Patterns, 32, 62, 76
  combining designs, 76
  contributes to texture, 65, 66,
    68, 72, 76
  for disguising architectural
    defects, 76
  in rugs, 76, 88, 92, 106, 118
  using effectively, 71, 72, 76
Pictures, 12, 58, 81, 94, 128,
    172, 173, 178, 214, 223
  arranging, 86, 115, 123, 169,
    170, 172–73, 221
  frames for, 214
  originals, 168
  prints, 168
  reproductions, 168, 170

yarn, *181*
Pillows, *21, 22, 27, 28, 43, 54,
177, 178, 214*
Plans, floor, *112, 115, 116, 122*
  bedroom, *116*
  groupings, *116, 120*
  kitchen, *120, 122*
  living room, *116*
  room dimensions, *120*
Plants, house, *79, 138, 151, 157,
166, 170, 178, 180, 182,
185*

Playrooms. *See* Family rooms

Queen Anne style, *25, 96, 98*

Rococo style, *23*
Room dividers, *232*
Rosewood furniture, *99, 100,
101*
Rubber tile flooring, *86*
Rugs, *30, 78, 86, 92, 94*
  area, *12, 59, 62, 86, 92*
  Aubusson, *92*
  bathroom, *180, 182*
  braided, *91, 94*
  and color schemes, *46, 86, 88,*

94
  crocheted, *94*
  cross-stitch, *94*
  hand-hooked, *94*
  lower-priced, *94*
  needlepoint, *94, 178*
  Oriental, *71, 76, 92*
    Persian, *92*
    Turkestan, *92*
    Turkish, *92*
  patterned, *25, 76, 88, 92, 106,
118*
  room dimensions and, *72, 88*
  room-size, *86, 89, 92*
  Scandinavian or rya, *94*
  shag, *28, 67, 83*
  for wall hangings, *68, 92, 216*
  See also Carpets
Rush, texture of, *72*

Satin
  texture of, *65*
  for upholstery, *108*
Satinwood furniture, *99, 100*
Screens, folding, *50, 62, 68, 120,
202, 214, 216*
Sewing room, In-a-wall, *232*
Shelves, *71, 125, 127, 134, 151,
174, 180, 212, 226*
  See also Walls, systems
Sheraton furniture, *10, 56, 99*
Shutters, *68, 92, 146, 155, 156,
164, 216*
Silk
  for braided rugs, *94*
  for draperies, *148*
  texture of, *66, 68*
  for upholstery, *108*
Slate
  flooring, *78, 80*
  -topped coffee table, *190*
Slipcovers, *102, 108*
Sofas, *101, 104*
  bed, *19, 27, 102, 118*
  Lawson, *91*
  love seats, *102, 127*
  Sheraton, *10*
  sectional type, *102*
  size of, *102*
Spanish style, *98*
Statuettes and figurines
  Mexican terra-cotta, *12*
  Staffordshire, *175*
Stenciling, *234, 238, 240*
Storage, *118, 202, 214, 216,
218*
  bathroom, *206*
  bedroom, *214*
  child's bedroom, *210, 234*
  closets

  installing extra, *200*
    organizing, *200*
  free-standing units, *125*
  nursery, *208*
  pegboard, *202, 208*
  of table settings, *232*
  wall systems, *174, 200, 202,
204, 217*
Straw, texture of, *72*
Synthetic fibers
  for carpets and rugs, *89, 91,
94*
  for draperies, *148*
  texture of, *68*
  for upholstery, *28, 106–8*

Table settings, *186, 190, 196*
  accessories, *192, 194, 199*
  buffet, *194, 198*
  candles, *198*
  centerpieces, *192, 195, 198*
  coverings, *195, 198*
  formal dinner, *196*
  informal dinner, *196*
  luncheon, *196*
  mood in, *199*
  napkins, *198*
  placemats, *188*
  storing, *232*
  See also Dinnerware; Flatware;
Glassware
Tables, *212*
  antiqued, *226*
  coffee, *19, 40, 57, 103, 115,
120, 124, 190*
  dropleaf, *220*
  end, *120*
  felt-covered, *21, 68*
  French provincial, *222*
  glass-topped, *42, 67, 106, 112,
218, 226*

lime-slice, *104*
marble-topped, *199*
nesting, *240*
pedestal, *192*
plastic cube, *51, 103*
round, *71, 116*
tea, *25*
tilt-top, *10*
trunk used for, *216*
unpainted, *108*
wicker, *236*

Taste in decorating, cultivating,
    26, 32
  learning from nature, *26*
Textures, *32, 62*
  in carpeting, *88*
  color and, *44, 65, 68, 72*
  combining, *65, 72*
  effects of, *62, 72*
  in fabric trimmings, *72*
  in fabrics, *66*
  in hard flooring, *66*
  light and, *44, 62, 65*
  look of, *65*
  in masonry, *66*
  need for balance of, *62, 67*
  in paint, *66*
  patterns can contribute to, *65,
      68, 72, 76*
  use of touch and, *62, 65*
  straw, cane, rush, *72*
  all coverings, *66*
  es can contribute to, *65*

  60, 238
  glazed, for flooring,
    5, 80

  for flooring, *68,*

  flooring
    , 183

  texture of, *65*

  e. *See* Fur-
  ered

Valances
  curtains, *150, 164*
  for draperies, *149, 154, 161,
      164, 238*
  for windows, *146, 150, 162,
      163*
Velvet
  texture of, *65*
  for upholstery, *106*
Victorian style, *100, 158, 197*
  colors of, *61*
Vinyl flooring, *59, 84, 86, 91,
      127, 227, 234, 236*
  asbestos tile, *84, 86*
  cork tile, -coated, *84, 111*
  sheet, *84*
    cushioned, *84*
    embossed, *84*
    inlaid, *84*
    rotogravure, *84*
  solid tile, *55, 75, 76, 79, 84,
      217, 218, 220*

Wallpaper, *68, 71, 75, 212, 214,
      216, 222, 223, 236*
  and ceilings, *76*
  designs, *76*
  prepasted, *68, 224*
  texture of, *65, 66*
Walls
  brick, *16, 19, 62, 66, 217*
  broken up, *222*
  coverings for, *15, 16, 28, 66,
      68, 72, 79, 216, 218,
      224, 238*
  hangings for, *27, 68, 92, 216*
  masonry on, *62, 66*
  plank, *223*
  prefinished panelling for, *28,
      32, 59, 66, 67, 72, 76,
      86, 101, 123, 216, 222*
  systems, *174, 200, 202, 204,
      217*
  texture on, *65, 66, 68*
  textured paint for, *66*
  window, *28, 32, 144, 148,
      155*
Walnut furniture, *98*
Weaves, contribute to texture,
    65, 66, 68
Windows, *30, 120, 142, 146,
      150, 151, 154, 156, 157,
      158, 159, 161, 162, 163,
      228*
  air conditioners in, *144, 152*
  bay, *152, 164*
  blinds for
    rollup matchstick, *83*
    split bamboo, *62, 162, 164*
    Venetian, *81, 154, 156, 158,*

  162, 230
  bow, *30, 164*
  clerestory, *32, 138, 148, 156*
  dormer, *163*
  double-hung, *148, 164*
  frosted glass, *162*
  measuring, *165*
  molding for, *142, 158, 162,
      214*
  picture, *148*
  problem, solutions for, *144,
      148, 152, 156, 161*
  screens, *157*
  shades, *28, 142, 148, 150*
    Austrian, *115, 154*
    designs on, *21, 46, 68, 116
        154, 158, 159, 162*
    Roman, *154, 162, 163*
  shutters, *92, 146, 155, 156,
      164, 216*
  stained glass panel, *159, 228*
  treatment for, choosing, *142,
      144*
  valances and cornices for, *146,
      150, 162, 163*
  walls, *28, 32, 144, 148, 155*
  wide or double, *164*
  See also Curtains; Draperies
Windsor chair, *96, 99*
Wood
  as a color, *44, 48*
  flooring, *66, 80–81, 222*
  furniture, *102, 108, 110*
    distressed, *110*
    plastic-laminate tops on,
        110, 230
    substitutes, *110*
    veneers, *108, 110*

  parquet flooring, *80*
  prefinished wall paneling of,
      *28, 32, 59, 66, 67, 72,
      76, 86, 101, 123, 216,
      222*
  texture and, *65, 72*
  See also individual kinds
Wool
  for carpets and rugs, *88–89,
      91, 92, 94*
  texture of, *65, 66*
  for upholstery, *106*